How To Rear Infants

BY

DR. JACK HYLES

Pastor
First Baptist Church
Hammond, Indiana

HYLES-ANDERSON PUBLISHERS

HAMMOND, INDIANA

Printed in the United States of America

FOREWORD

In 1974 my book HOW TO REAR CHILDREN was published. Its first offspring was born in 1978 and was named HOW TO REAR TEENAGERS. Soon I began to travail again, realizing that perhaps the most important time in the molding of a child's character was his infancy. As a result of these labors was born HOW TO REAR INFANTS, which I lovingly and prayerfully present to those excited young couples who are eagerly anticipating the joys and responsibilities of parenthood.

Dr. Jack Hyles

DEDICATION

Lovingly dedicated to that faithful and loyal army of ladies who work in the nursery at First Baptist Church of Hammond, Indiana, who do so much for so many so unselfishly. Unknown to us but known to our Heavenly Father and recorded in His books are the names of the thousands of people who have been converted because of the contribution made to our services by these dear servants of God. Hence the author dedicates this manuscript to:

Glendarae Lanoue—*Nursery Director*

Kaye Andrews	Debbie Donley
Judy Anderson	Jeanne Donovan
Bette Atkinson	Betty Elwell
Pat Atkinson	Alechia Evans
Ruth Atkinson	Rose Farley
Linda Ault	Barbara Farmer
Sudie Beasley	Doris Fink
Cindy Blackburn	Karen Fink
Jan Brown	Marjean Finn
Susan Brubaker	Kathy Fleming
Jackie Bryant	Linda Flesher
Terry Buchholz	Margaret Foutch
Katrina Bullard	Cassie Franklin
Flo Burns	Karen Gehling
Kris Burr	Connie Gardner
Peggy Carter	Tricia Giffin
Beverly Clark	Gail Gilley
Elaine Colbert	Trudy Glover
Jean Colbert	Bettie Goldsborough
Pam Connor	Carla Gomez
Glenda Coon	Chris Hall
Darlene Corbin	Pat Hamilton
Susan Crislip	Patsy Harrington
Mary Deneve	Diane Harris

Judy Hayes
Peggy Hayes
Barbara Heatherly
Kay Hedge
Susie Heidenreich
Kathy Hiles
Sarah Holeman
Hazel Hotkiewicz
Carol Huckins
Sue Huey
Nancy Hulet
Karen Hurley
Barbara Jones
Delores Jones
Joyce Jones
Marianne Jones
Marilyn Jorgensen
Linda Kelly
Dianna Kendrick
Sharmaine Kennedy
Georgia Kirk
Kathy Klingensmith
Connie Kurtz
Barbara Kuykendall
Doris Lail
Teresa Lands
Judy Leib
Linda Lockhart
Leslie Lundy
Jillana Mann
Joan Marker
Ruth Minton
Sue Minton
Cora Moake
Barbara Mock
Vickie Mooney
Kathy Moore

Donna Moors
Glenda Morgan
Bea Mulligan
Pat Mundt
Christine McClain
Nancy Nack
Karen Nisely
Neva Norrell
Donna Nottoli
Dian Ogle
Jan Olenhouse
Jeri Osborn
Carol Overstreet
Linda Parker
Sandy Perkins
Debbi Petropoulos
Erlene Phelps
Bonnie Pickering
Dawn Pidkaminy
Stephanie Potter
Patricia Powell
Evelyn Poynter
Denise Preston
Sally Pruitt
Dianna Pulliam
Jeanne Ray
Robin Rhoades
Pam Rhodes
Vicki Riggle
Pat Roundtree
Judy Rushing
Alma Scales
Ann Seifreid
Jenny Seward
Cindy Shelar
Rose Shepherd
Frances Shirley

Launa Shoemaker
Sandy Simcox
Jan Simpson
Pat Sinclair
Karey Sisson
Vicky Skow
Ann Smith
Char Smith
Doris Smith
Sherrie Snavely
Leah Snow
Tina Sonday
Candy Spear
Priscilla Staab
Lorry Steen
Sandy Stiller
Liz Stombaugh
Maxine Stromberg
Rhonda Talley
Maribeth Taylor
Joyce Tesseneer
Vicki Tevault
Connie VanWienen
Gayle Vargo
Jan Vogel
Sheryl Vyborny
Denise Walters
Deborah Watts
Marcia Weber
Connie Weddell
Donna Weddell
Roberta Wertz
Ginny Wilson
Mary Pat Wilson
Jean Wolfe
Diane Wood
Mary Young

ABOUT THE AUTHOR

Jack Hyles began preaching at the age of 19 and has pastored for over 30 years. These pastorates include churches that varied in membership from 19 to over 48,000. All of these pastorates, other than the present one, were in the state of Texas: First, the Marris Chapel Baptist Church of Bogata, Texas; then to the Grange Hall Baptist Church in Marshall, Texas; from there to the Southside Baptist Church of Henderson, Texas; and then to the Miller Road Baptist Church of Garland, Texas. He pastored the Miller Road Baptist Church for 7 years and saw this church, under the Lord, grow from a membership of 19 to over 4,000. It was from the Miller Road Baptist Church that he was called to his present pastorate at the First Baptist Church in Hammond, Indiana.

Dr. Hyles has been Pastor of the First Baptist Church since August, 1959. This church has a membership of over 48,000 and has averaged for the past 4 years over 23,000 conversions and 7,000 baptisms per year. For many years the church has been acclaimed to have the "World's Largest Sunday School." During Dr. Hyles' ministry the First Baptist Church has increased in property evaluation to over $21,000,000.

Besides his position as Pastor, Dr. Hyles is Superintendent of Hammond Baptist Schools—Hammond Baptist Grade School, Hammond Baptist Junior High School, Hammond Baptist High School, and Hammond City Baptist High School—and Founder of Hyles-Anderson College. The College, now in its 7th year, matriculated over 1,500 students this year. It is housed in a beautiful 76-acre campus with buildings valued at $10 million. (All of the schools are operated by the First

Baptist Church and are housed in separate facilities away from the church property.) Dr. Hyles has served as President of the Baptist Bible College in Denver, Colorado. He is now Assistant Editor-Conference Director of the SWORD OF THE LORD, America's foremost Christian weekly. He also serves as a Vice-President of the Sword of the Lord Foundation.

Dr. Hyles is the author of 27 books and pamphlets exceeding over 5 million copies in sales. One long-play record by Dr. Hyles is also available, "Let's Go Soul Winning" (awarded by the Evangelical Film Foundation an Oscar as the outstanding talk record of 1967), as well as many tape-recorded sermons.

Dr. Hyles' experience covers numerous evangelistic campaigns, Bible Conferences, etc. He has preached in virtually every state of the Union and in many foreign countries. His annual Pastors' School attracts preachers from every state and many foreign countries. More than 3,600 registrants attend each year.

TABLE OF CONTENTS

Chapter One

PREPARING FOR THE BABY

Someone is coming to live in your home. Serious and loving preparations should be made for his arrival.

The wise couple will realize that every aspect of their lives is about to change. They should discard the stereotype picture of parenthood which emphasizes the joys, thrills and excitements and de-emphasizes the problems that are sure to arise. If these problems are predicted, and if proper preparation is made for them, a couple will not find themselves disappointed and disillusioned by parenthood. Such preparation not only can avoid domestic strife and marital problems, but it can bring the parents even closer to each other, and the baby can be a reconciler rather than a divider. Several types of preparation should be made.

1. *The parents should determine that the baby will not come between them.* Definite plans should be made so that there will be ample time for Mom and Dad to be alone. They must be aware that before the first baby arrives, they have been alone together, and that now a very attractive and enticing intruder is about to enter on the scene. Before he enters, they must both promise and plan to spend time alone together after he arrives. They must plan to continue to be sweethearts. They must also face the reality that the baby is only theirs on loan for a few years. In 18 or 20 years he will be gone, and Mom and Dad will still have each other. They must purposely plan to be closer to each other on the day of his departure than on the day of his

arrival. There are just a few hours between the bassinet and the honeymoon suite, between the playpen and the college dormitory; between the moment that the proud parents observe the nurse arriving with their new loved one and the moment that together they watch daughter disappear as she leaves the marriage altar. Proper preparation before the baby's arrival can insure that both his coming and leaving will bring Mom and Dad closer together.

2. *The couple should prepare for help when the baby arrives.* When Mother and child return from the hospital some assistance will be needed for at least a few days. Careful planning is important for you, for your child, and for the relationship between the two of you. Whatever assistance is secured and arrangements are made, it is vital that you realize that the little one that is coming is YOUR baby and YOUR responsibility. This outside help that comes in must not interfere with the quick adjustment of parents and child and must not retard that spontaneous warmth and affection that is God-given. DO NOT BRING SOMEONE IN TO TAKE CARE OF THE CHILD! Let the assistance be in caring for the meals, the house, etc. This will enable the parents to give more time to the baby and to other children in the family. Too much emphasis could not be given to the fact that the parents should take care of the child. Outside assistance could take care of cleaning, cooking, shopping, and other household responsibilities. Spend your time giving assurance to older children, becoming acquainted with the baby, and offering each other the security of increased love. It is not necessary that the parents employ an experienced nurse to come and care for the baby. It is not necessary that Grandmother be brought in to take care

of the baby. This is not to say that Grandmother should not be the one chosen to assist, but whoever it is should confine his or her duties to performing a task that will free the parents so they can spend more time with their new arrival, with each other and with other children. More than your baby needs professional care, he needs you. God has placed emotional appetites within the breast of that little one that can be satisfied only by the ones who gave him life. No one else can substitute. In some cases, this may require a frank talk with Grandmother and Grandfather who oftentimes will remind you that they have raised several children of their own and that they are experts in the field. No such expertise can take the place of the ones who gave life to this winsome little intruder. No amount of experience can take the place of maternal and, yes, paternal instinct and love.

It might even be wise for Dad to take part or all of his vacation for this little period of adjustment. Bear in mind, after marriage, there was the honeymoon so the couple could get to know each other better and adjust and blend. Perhaps at the coming of a child there should be a "little honeymoon" where Mom and Dad and baby can learn to adjust to each other.

The wise grandparents will allow for such time. They will give themselves to making it easier and more conducive for the new unit to become adjusted. This is difficult, for there is the unique joy and thrill given to grandparents upon the arrival of their grandchildren. How proud they are! How boastful they feel! This is certainly a natural reaction.

This excitement, however, should be properly channeled. Perhaps it would be good for the grandparent to pause and remember. Then he may adjust his behavior to that which he once wanted from his own parents when his children were born.

If a couple cannot afford a nurse or a housekeeper, and if relatives are not available or their coming would cause problems, there is yet another place where a mother can turn for help. She could turn to her own husband. Many husbands take vacations during the first days after the baby comes home, and they clean, cook, wash, and in general, help to free the new mother to become adjusted with her baby. One thing is often overlooked, and that is, just as there is a mother instinct, there is also a father instinct. In some cases, perhaps Dad is the best help of all!

3. *Preparation should be made for the feeding of the baby.* Serious discussion and consideration should be given to breast feeding or bottle feeding. Do not wait until the last moment to make this decision. Sometimes the decision is not made until the baby is born, and maybe even in the delivery room the doctor will ask for a decision. This is not the time to decide. Mom and Dad should have spent hours carefully weighing the pros and cons of breast feeding.

In some cases, bottle feeding is best. However, it is the opinion of this author that there are many advantages derived from breast feeding. In the first place, there is the instinctive desire in the baby to be close to the body of the mother. This instinct carries with it a desire to feel and see the face and to hear Mother's voice. These appetites can be satisfied as the child spends hours with Mother and develops a closeness that cannot be developed when Mother props a bottle on a pillow beside the baby and goes into the other room to watch television, or for that matter, to perform routine chores. If for any reason breast feeding is impossible, I strongly advise the mother (or father) to hold the baby while feeding him, especially in the early days of his life. Close contact is very important!

The child could be given a formula occasionally, even though the mother is breast feeding. This will give Dad an opportunity to feed the baby and will also provide a gradual process of weaning.

Another advantage of breast feeding is that it insures the proper temperature for the baby's milk. It also prevents the sour smell when the baby is burped. It insures the fact that the diet has been provided by God rather than by man. It also helps to prevent dental problems later in life, for the breast is an aid in preventing the baby in becoming a tongue thruster. It also enables the proper supply of milk to be available. It certainly is easier for the night feedings (especially for Dad!). Breast feeding usually makes Mother less tense, for it guarantees that she will have a time to relax periodically during some very busy days of her life.

I have been pastoring over 30 years. I have never met a mother who regretted breast feeding her baby. Occasionally I have talked with mothers who wished they had done so. Let me hasten to stress, however, that it is not wrong or sinful to bottle feed the baby. There are some cases (though very rare) when the mother cannot provide enough milk. Then there are some mothers who are so emotionally tense that it would not be healthy for the baby to be breast fed. It is, however, usually best for the baby to be fed from his mother's breast so he can feel the warmth from her body, the touch of her hand, the contour of her face and where he can hear her voice as she speaks and sings to him.

A study was once made which arrived at the conclusion that puppy dogs who were weaned too soon became destructive, especially with their mouths, and that this carried even into their adulthood. These dogs who were weaned prematurely chewed up table legs, chairs, beds, curtains throughout their lives. On the other hand, the dogs that were weaned naturally and later were not destructive. They seemed to be more contented than those who were prematurely weaned.

Before the baby arrives, the parents should sit down and talk and pray together. They should seek God's will concerning the child's feeding. They should secure whatever facts are available on the subject. If there is a disagreement, the mother's opinion should be the most important, for if the mother were to breast feed the child against her own wishes, it could cause more harm than good.

4. *Older children must be prepared for the baby's coming.* Let me hasten to say in the beginning that this preparation should not be overdone. Some parents become extravagant in their expenditure of money for purchasing gifts for the older children. This is not wise. The children cannot be prepared with presents, things, material objects. They, like Dad, must be assured that the coming of the baby will not lessen their importance in the family, but rather increase it. They must realize that the baby will have a place of his own and that he will be an important part of the family, but that his place has nothing to do with the place of the other children. Each child has the place he has always had and is as important or more so than he was prior to the baby's arrival. Wise parents will see to it that the older child has some of their attention. This attention should not be demanded or even sought, for it is unwise for a child to feel that he must demand attention in order to get it. In some cases he will even resort to misbehavior to get this attention. The parents should explain to the child that there is a

unique love for him that can never be diminished or threatened by the coming of another human being into the home. The love that the parent has for the older child is unique because he is unique; it is different because he is different. He must be led to believe that he has a special place in the home that no one can fill. The parents, however, should realize that it is normal and natural for the older child to have some degree of dislike about the idea of competition coming into the home. Because of this, the parents must prepare him before the baby comes by letting him know that he has a place no one can fill and that the baby will provide no competition whatsoever. Again, don't overdo it. Don't try to buy him off with expensive gifts. Rather, with calm assurance give him some undivided attention without his having to demand it to let him know that he will become even more important. Let him know that you will need help—his help—in rearing the baby. Remind him that God has given him to you as a helper during this time. Remind him that he is to be an example and a pattern to whom the baby can look. Remind him that he will be the baby's hero. Remind him that you had him first, and that will always make him a very special person. Take time to cuddle the older child, especially after the baby comes. Be sure he gets his share of attention. Tell him that the baby is coming. Get him excited about it. Tell him some things he can do to prepare. Let him be part of the family preparation. Mother, while you are in the hospital, call home several times, especially after the birth of the baby, and tell the child at home that you have already told the baby how wonderful he is! As soon as possible, introduce the baby to the older child. As you do, tell the baby what a wonderful brother or sister he has. Let the older child become a part of the total happening.

It should also be stressed to the older child that the baby will not be able to play immediately. He should be made aware that the baby is fragile and must be treated carefully for a few months.

The mother should realize that the child has the same problem that Dad has. Both Dad and child can feel threatened. The wise mother will provide ample security and assurance to these who love her and who need her love in a unique way to them. Never scold the child if he seems to be jealous. Overwhelm him with the positive; do not confront him with the negative.

This is a vital part in preparing for the baby. Done properly, it can provide an even happier home. Done carelessly or not done at all, it can provide emotional and psychological marks on the lives of parents and children that will never leave.

5. *The parents should prepare for the baby's coming by the choosing of a name.* It is tremendously important that care and prayer be a part of the choosing of a name for the baby. Too many of us think of names as being mere identification tags, but the right name can have a lifetime effect on the new human being that you are about to bring into the world.

In ancient times each person was given but one name and that name usually was a descriptive one that was hand tailored to fit. These names were chosen much like nicknames are chosen now; such as, "Red," "Slim," "Rusty," "Pleasant," "Grace," "Hope," etc. Sometimes these names were related to some circumstance surrounding birth or some quality of character or some achievements performed later in life. For example, Adam means "formed of red earth." Andrew means "manly." Naomi means "pleasant."

Later it became popular to name babies after outstanding characters. This meant that many people had the same names. Hence, people began giving family names and later, even middle names. Family names were usually derived from occupations, trades, local events or local surroundings. Here is a fellow, for example, who is named Bill. He is tall, so he would be called Bill Tall. There might be a Bill Short or a Bill Strong.

As parents choose the name for a child, there are several things that should be considered. Remember that the name given to the child will be a part of his identity for life. It can affect his personality; it can affect his security; it can even affect his acceptance by other people and his popularity. It could even adversely affect his opportunities for success in his chosen profession. Some parents try to be clever in naming their children and often cause much harm later in life. For example, if the last name is Green, it would be unwise to name the child Kelly, for no one would want to go through life with the name Kelly Green. If the family name is Hill, parents should resist the temptation to be clever by naming the child Ima, for who would want to be called Ima Hill for lifetime!

Care should be taken to be sure that the child's name distinquishes his sex. For example, in some countries a boy could be appropriately named Francis Jean or even Joyce, but in other countries this is not appropriate, for these are names uniquely suited and given to girls.

Often religion should affect the choice of the name for the baby. Catholic children are often given the name of a saint. Jewish children are usually named for some member of the family who has passed away. Christian children are often given Bible names such as Jacob, Joseph, John, James,

David, Stephen, etc.

It is wise to consider rhythm in naming the child. It is usually best when the surname has only one syllable such as Smith that the given name has two or more syllables such as Bobby Jones, Johnny Smith, Betty Cook, etc. When the surname has two syllables such as Parker, Little, etc., a three-syllable first name is often suitable such as Anthony Roberts, Melinda Johnson. If the surname has three syllables, it is good for the first name to have only one or two syllables such as John Peabody, Susie Rosenbloom, etc. A good rule to follow is this: The given name and surname should have a different number of syllables. Now this is not always the case and certainly not a fast rule, but simply a guideline.

In naming a baby the parents should also consider the potential nicknames derived from the given name. Robert is usually called Bob, Richard is usually called Dick, etc. Think of all the possible nicknames that people (especially children) could devise.

Also, consider the danger of naming a child after someone whose footsteps you want him to follow. For example, it would be unwise to name a child George Washington, expecting him to become president someday; or Babe Ruth, expecting him to become a baseball star. Parents should not determine the vocation that their children pursue. They should not give them a name with the expectancy of their becoming a likeness of their namesake. Now, it would be fine for someone to name a child Stephen, in hopes that he will have the courage of Stephen; or John, in hopes that he will be as faithful as John, but care should be taken not to expect the child to follow in professional footprints.

Do not leave the child with a name that is a

novelty. For example, I know a fine man whose name is Forrest Ranger.

Choose a name, but then say the name over and over again to make sure it will not be a cause for embarrassment in years to come.

Be extra careful to look into the meaning of names before you name a child. For example, you would not want to choose a name which means "dark" for a child who is of light complexion, or a name which means "small" or "little" for a child who may someday become huge.

Remember that you are doing your child a favor if you give him a name he will enjoy. Though he can legally change his name, usually he will not. He will bless you if you give him a name that is pleasant to the ear and positive in its impressions.

FOLLOWING ARE THE MEANINGS OF SOME NAMES FOR BOYS:

Aaron—a mountain of strength; he who is exalted

Adolph—a noble helper

Adrian—brave

Allan—harmony, graceful

Albert—intelligent, bright

Alexander—a helper of men; a protector

Alvin—a friend to everybody

Andrew—manly

Anthony—graceful, valuable

Arnold—strong as an eagle

Arthur—strong as a bear; strong as a rock

Arvin—a friend of people

Asa—physician

Aubrey—chief who is fair-haired, rich and mighty

Austin—renowned

Baldwin—prince friend

Barry—son of Harry; also spear

Bart—ploughman

Baruch—blessed

Basil—kingly

Ben—blessed

Benjamin—son of right hand

Bernard—bold as a bear

Bertrum—fair and pure

Boris—a fighter

Boyd—light-haired

Brian—strong

Brice—ambitious; alert

Byron—a clear discerner

Caleb—bold

Carl—strong; manly

Chalmer—king of the household

Charles—manly; of great strength

Chester—fortified

Christopher—Christ-bearer

Clarence—bright; illustrious

Clark—scholarly

Clement—mild, kind

Conrad—wise counselor

Curt or Curtis—courteous

Dallas—skilled

Daniel—God is my judge

Darcy—stronghold

Darrell—beloved

Darren—loved

David—beloved

Davin—the bright one

Dennis—lover of fine wines

Dillon—faithful

Dominick—born on Sunday

Douglas—dark

Drew—skilled and honest

Druce—wise man

Duane—singing

Duke—leader

Durand—enduring

Durwin—dear friend

Dustin—stronghearted leader

Dwight—light

Edgar—good spearman

Edmond—blessed peace; defender of happiness

Edward—happy guard; guardian of happiness

Edwin—rich friend or happy conqueror

Eldon—respected

Eldridge—wise adviser

Eli—highest

Elmer—noble

Elmo—friendly

Emel—industrious

Emery—ambitious

Enoch—dedicated; educated

Eric—lord; hero

Ernest—serious; sincere

Ethan—strength; power

Eugene—well born

Ezra—helper

Farrell—valiant

Felix—happy

Fergus—strong; fierce

Forest—from wooder country

Forestor—keeper of the preservation

Frank—free; courageous

Frederick—peaceful

Gabriel—God is mighty

Gale—lively

Galen—healer

Gardiner—flower lover

Garett—mighty sword

Garner—the defender

Garrick—mighty warrior

Garth—ground keeper

Garvin—friend

Gaylord—joyous

Gene—noble; well born

George—farmer

Gifford—gift

Gilbert—pledge

Gilroy—the king's faithful servant

Godfrey—God's peace

Godwin—beloved of God; a conqueror for God; divine friend

Gordon—a fine man; a strong man

Graham—stern; gloomy; a frowner

Grant—brave

Gregory—watchman

Griffith—red-haired; ruddy

Gunter—bold warrior

Guy—guide; leader, director

Gustave—noble

Harold—leader of the army

Hans or Hansel—a gift from the Lord

Harrison—son of Henry

Harry—son of Henry

Henry—ruler at home

Herbert—great fighter

Hermon—noble warrior

Herwin—a lover of battle or a friend

Hilary—cheerful; merry

Hilliard—protector

Hiram—most exalted; most noble

Holden—kind

Homer—pledge

Hosea—salvation

Houston—from a mountain town

Hoyt—of shining mind

Hubert—a bright mind

Hugh—intelligent; thoughtful; wise; high; lofty

Hume—lover of home

Humphrey—protector of the home

Hyman—masculine

Irvin—friend of the sea

Isaac—laughing

Jack—God's gracious gift

Jason—healer

Jay—lively

Jeffrey—joyful peace

Jeremiah—exalted of the Lord

Jeremy—exalted of the Lord

Jerome—holy

Jesse—God's gift

Jethro—outstanding

Joab—praise the Lord

Job—one who mourns; one who is persecuted

Joel—he who wills or commands

John—God's gracious gift; grace

Jonah—peace or dove

Jonathan—gift of the Lord

Joshua—saviour or deliverer

Joses—helped by the Lord

Junius—born in June

Kemp—a soldier; champion at arms

Kendall—chief of the valley

Kenneth—good-looking

Kerby—from the church village

Kervin—noble; kind; friendly; handsome

Kimbal—brave

Kirk—living close to the church

Knute—kind

Kyle—fair and handsome

Lambert—innocence

Lance—servant

Lang—tall

Lawrence—laurel; crowned with honor

Lawton—man of refinement

Leland—of the lowlands

Lemuel—consecrated to God

Leo—brave as a lion

Leroy—the king

Ludwig—safeguard; good leader

Luther—famous warrior

Lyle—from the island

Madison—mighty

Malcolm—dove

Manuel—God with us

Mark—brilliant; polished; born in month of March

Martin—marshall; warlike

Matthew—gift of the Lord

Maurice—dark complexion

Maynard—strong and mighty

Medwin—strong friend

Meredith—sea protector

Micah—like unto the Lord

Michael—God-like

Miles—soldier

Mordecai—a wise counselor

Myron—myhr; a sweet smell

Nathan—gift of God

Nathaniel—gift of God

Neal—champion

Neil—champion; of a dark complexion

Nestor—continual wisdom

Noah—consolation; peace

Noble—to be admired; renowned

Nolan—renowned; to be admired

Norman—man from the north

Nortan—from the north place

Odel—wealthy man

Oliver—oliver tree; symbol of peace

Oscar—bounding warrior; he who leaps to the fight

Osborne—divinely strong

Osmond—protected by God

Otis—quick to hear

Otto—wealthy; a mountain

Parry—protector

Parker—keeper of the parks

Patrick—noble

Paul—little; small; gentle

Peter—little rock

Philbert—radiant soul

Philip—lover of horses

Powell—alert

Preston—of the priest's place

Prior—superior

Proctor—leader

Quartus—fourth son

Quentin—born

Radburn—he lives by the red brook

Radcliff—from the red cliff

Radford—by the red valley

Raymond—quiet; peaceful; wise protector

Redmond—adviser

Regan—royal

Reginald—mighty ruler

Ruben—behold, a son

Rex—king

Richard—generous; benevolent; liberal; wealthy

Richmond—powerful protector

Robert—bright shining; famous

Roderick—generous counselor; famous king

Rodney—famous in counsel

Rodger—famous warrior

Russell—red-haired

Samuel—asked of God

Saul—longed for; desired; asked of the Lord

Scott—a Scotsman

Shawn—God's gracious gift; grace

Seth—chosen

Sewell—victorious at sea

Shane—God's gracious gift; grace

Sherwin—true friend

Sigmund—victorious protector

Sinclair—saintly; shining

Sloan—warrior

Solomon—peaceful

Sprague—quick

Standley—the pride of the camp

Stephen—a crown

Sterling—honest; genuine

Stewart—keeper of the estate

Sumner—one who summons and calls

Sutton—from the south of town

Tate—cheerful

Tadis—son of David

Ted—happy guard; guardian of happiness

Terence—tender

Thad or Thadeus—praise

Theodore—gift of God

Thomas—a twin

Timothy—one who honors God

Titus—safe or saved

Tobias—goodness of God

Tony—graceful; valuable

Townsend—from the end of town

Tracey—a brave protector

Trent—swift

Truman—a faithful man

Tyler—a maker of tiles or bricks

Tyson—a German son

Val—might; power

Vance—son of a famous family

Victor—conqueror

Vaughan—small

Vernon—flourishing; green

Vincent—the conqueror

Vincin—the conqueror's son

Virgil—strong; flourishing

Wade—mover or wanderer

Waldo—mighty; powerful

Wallace—from Wales; a foreigner

Walter—chief of an army; woodmaster

Ward—watchman; guardian

Ware—always careful

Warner—protector

Warren—protecting friend

Webster—a weaver

Wendell—a wanderer

Wilfred—peaceful

William or Will—determined protector; protector of many; defender; shield

Winfred—friend or winner of peace

Winston—from the friendly town

Winthrop—from the friendly village

Willie—charming

Yancy—Englishman

York—sacred tree

Zachery—the Lord's remembrance

FOLLOWING ARE THE MEANINGS OF SOME NAMES FOR GIRLS:

Abby—sweet refuge

Abigail—her father's joy

Ada—significant; of great beauty; ornament; joyous; prosperous

Agatha—good

Agnes—pure; chaste; gentle

Aimeé—beloved

Alberta—bright; noble

Alda—rich

Alethea—truth

Alexis—helper of mankind

Alice—noble; illustrious; truthful

Aline—noble

Alma—fair

Althea—wholesome

Alvina—bright; joyous

Amanda—beloved

Amelia—busy; energetic; a good worker

Amy—beloved

Andrea—brave; noble

Angela—angelic

Anita—gracious; merciful

Ann—grace

Annabel—beautiful Ann

Arabella—sweet; a refuge

Aurella—golden hair

Aurora—dawn

Angie—angelic

Anya—grace

Ardis—fervent; zealous

Astra—like a star

Audrey—strong; noble

Barbara—a stranger

Beatrice—blessed; happy

Belinda—graceful in motion

Becky—see Rebecca

Beryl—gem

Bernice—she brings victory

Bona or Bonnie—good; fair

Beth—house of God

Beverly—a beaver meadow

Billie—wise protector

Bina—a princess

Blanche—fair; white

Bobbi—stranger; foreigner

Bonnie—sweet and good

Belinda—dark-haired; dark-eyed

Brenna—with black or raven hair

Bridget—strength

Candace—pure

Cara—friend

Carissa—graceful

Carla—strong

Carlotta—valiant

Carmel—God's fruitful field

Carmen—charming

Carol—joyous

Caroline—one who is strong

Carrie—one who is strong

Catherine—pure; virtuous

Cecelia—gray-eyed; musical

Celeste—heavenly

Chandra—she outshines the stars

Charissa—graceful

Charlene—stong

Charity—lovable

Charlotte—womanly

Charmaine—little song

Chloë—fresh; youthful

Christine—follower of Christ

Clara—shining; glorious; brilliant

Claribel—brightly fair

Clarice or Clarissa—fair; pure

Claudette or Claudia—lame

Clementine—mild in temper

Cleopatra—glory of her famous father

Coleen—a maid; little girl

Constance—stedfast; firm; unyielding

Cora—jewel of the sea

Corine—a maiden

Cornelia—symbol of royalty

Crystal—clear

Cynthia—from Mt. Cynthus; also, goddess of the moon

Darlene—dearly beloved

Davina—the loved

Dawn—daybreak; beginning

Deborah—industrious; active

Delilah—delicate

Delphine—a loving sister

Denise—god of wine and drama

Diana—clear; bright; the goddess of hunting

Dina—one who is judged and vindicated

Dolly—gift of God

Delores—sorrow

Donna—a lady

Dixie—girl of the south

Dione—daughter of heaven and earth

Dorcas—she who has beautiful eyes

Dorinda—a gift

Dulce—sweet

Drusilla—soft-eyed

Edith—happiness

Edna—pleasure

Eileen—light

Elaine—light

Eleanor—light

Elen—light

Elizabeth—oath of God

Eloise—much holiness

Elsa—cheer

Elvira—courage

Emily—busy; energetic

Ema—nurse

Earnestine—serious

Estele—a star

Esther—a star

Ethel—noble

Etta—ruler at home

Eudora—a beautiful gift

Eugenea—well born

Eunice—victorious

Eva—a mother; a life-giver

Evlina—pleasant

Evelyn—pleasant

Faith—a firm believer

Fanchette—free

Faustina—happy

Fay—a firm believer

Felecia—fortunate

Fern—sincere

Fidelia—of good character

Flavia—blonde

Flora or Florette—a flower

Florabel—a beautiful flower

Florence—prosperity

Frances or Francene—free; courageous; strong

Frieda—peaceful

Fritzie—peaceful ruler

Gail—see Abagail

Geraldine—spear power

Gladys—lame

Gloria—glory

Grace—kindness; patience

Gwendolyn—white-browed

Haidee—modest

Hannah—gracious; merciful

Harriet—rich and powerful

Hazel—one that sees God

Heather—lonely

Hedy—defense

Helen—light; bright dawn

Helga—holy

Henretta—ever rich and mighty

Hilda—battle maid

Holly—friendship and happiness

Hope—trust in the future

Hortence—a gardener

Huldah—quick; spritely

Ida—thristy

Imagine—beloved child; last-born

Ina—uncertain

Ines—pure

Irene—peace; iris; the rainbow; picture of beauty uniting earth and sky

Irma—friendship; fidelity

Jaquelin—supplanter

Jane—God's grace

Jean, Jeanette, Jennie, Jenny—God's grace

Jemina—a dove

Jenifer—white wave

Jessica or Jessie—wealthy

Jewell—life

Jill—soft-haired

Joy—gladness

Joyce—vivacious

Juanita—God's grace

Judith—one who praises

Julia—soft-haired

Justine—righteous

Karen—pure

Kathryn and Kathleen—little darling; pure; beautiful eyes

Lala—a tulip

Laura or Laurette—laurel; emblem of fame

Lavania—left-handed

Leah—weary

Leila—dark beauty

Lena—peace

Leona—lion

Letitia—joy, gladness

Lida—people's love

Lily or Linda—pretty

Lois—virtue

Loretta—emblem of fame

Louise—protector of the people

Lucretia—a good housewife

Lucia, Lucille, Lucinda, Lucy—light; born at daybreak

Lynn—a pool or lake

Mabel, Mabelle—fair one

May—weeping

Mae—weeping

Malvina—smooth forehead

Marcela—brave

Marcia—brave

Maria—merry

Marie, Marietta—distressed or tearful

Marilyn, Marlene—distressed or tearful

Maxine—the greatest

Maybelle—fair one

Melanie—black

Melinda—sweet as honey

Melissa—honey bee

Merie—blackbird

Mildred—gentle

Mina—beloved

Miranda—admirable

Mona—alone

Monica—one dwelling alone

Muriel—of sweet scent

Mira—weeping

Nada and Nadeen—hope

Nancy and Nanette—grace

Naomi—pleasant

Nina—small darling

Nola—honor

Norma—pattern; example

Octavia—the eighth born

Olga—righteous

Olive and Oliva—peace

Opal—hope

Palma—victory

Pamela—sweetness; a brunette

Patience—aflicted without complaint

Patricia—of noble birth

Paula and Pauline—gentle; little

Pearl—health and long life

Perpetua—lasting

Phoebe—radiant

Phyllis—a reed

Polly—bitter

Portia—safety

Priscilla—old-fashioned

Prudence—wisdom; discretion; knowledge

Rachel—innocence

Rebecca—one who snares men by her beauty

Regina—a queen

Renee—revived

Rhoda—a rose

Roberta—a shining counselor

Rosabel—fair rose

Roselyn, Rosalie and Rosalind—pretty as a rose

Rosemund—rose of the world

Rose—symbol of love

Rosemary—rose of the sea

Rowena—to acquire peace

Roxana—dawn

Ruby—contentment

Ruth—beauty

Sabina—chaste; religious

Sarah—a noble lady

Selma—fair

Sibyl—divine

Silvia—of the forest

Sophia—wise woman

Stella—a star

Stephanie—a crown

Susan, Susanne or Susette—a lily

Tabitha—beautiful eyes

Thalia—flourishing; blooming

Theresa—a harvester; beautiful

Thora—consecrated

Ursella—a little bear

Valerie—healthy

Verna—youthful

Victoria—conqueror

Viola and Violet—pretty; modest

Virginia—a virgin; chaste

Vivian—lively; merry

Yvonne—God's grace or gift

Zora—dawn

The wise parent will carefully and prayerfully choose a name. That name may be a dream within the parent's breast. It may be a lovely description of the child as the parent sees him. Remember, it is a gift given by the parents to the child that is rarely ever returned.

Chapter Two

THE DAYS AT THE HOSPITAL

1. *Extra care should be taken when there are already other children.* Junior has been the only child for a long time. Suddenly a new baby appears. The first child soon discovers that his mother has another one. This new one takes most of her time and most of her affection. He has been exiled from his mother while she was in the hospital. Now the new baby moves into her bedroom, feeds from her breast, receives most of her attention, and is the object of most of her affection. The little intruder receives most of the hugs and most of the loving talk from Mother. Jealousy soon creeps in. Mother is weak and unable to run the house. It is all she can do to care for her little one. She cannot possibly give her first child his usual attention. She cannot eat with him, play with him or spend time with him as she could before the new arrival. The child feels neglected. It is a sudden thing. No longer is he the most important and the most attended. He feels wronged by his mother, and he is jealous of the baby. He feels abandoned and isolated. Maybe he has been over loved previously and now suddenly he who was perhaps even spoiled feels that he is all alone in the world.

When the newborn begins to smile for the first time and do cute little things and learn new skills, the older child becomes more frightened and more jealous. He once had it all; now he has only a part. He will never have their undivided love again. He will never receive what he once had—the place of being the only loved one in his parents' hearts. This may result in his wanting to attack verbally the younger child. This is especially true when the older child is the first child. A second child never had *all* of the attention. Hence, he will not be as jealous as was the first child. The wise parent will take extra care to see that the first child is given extra attention and extra love during these days of adjustment.

Surveys have proven that in a two-child family, the oldest is always more jealous and selfish. He is also more likely to be reared "according to the book," which means he will be more anxious and more restless. The second child comes when the parents are more oriented in rearing children and more relaxed. Studies show that the older child is more jealous and selfish, and the second child is happier. The first child was trained more severely than the second. He was weaned earlier than the second. He started toilet training earlier than the second, and in general, received more attention than the second child. Because he did receive more attention, he has more attention to miss when the second child appears. Often the first child will try to hit the baby, take his bottle, shove the baby out of Mother's lap, say he doesn't like the baby, or call the baby a puppy. Sometimes the child will even suggest that the baby be given back or sent back to whoever sent it. Some first children even learn to resent the mother. Often the older child becomes sullen and may even hit or kick the mother while she is nursing the baby. This hostility toward the mother is a rare thing, but it does happen. If the first child is very young when his brother or sister arrives, he himself may want to go back to being treated like a baby. He may want to go back to the bottle again or want to stay home from school or to soil or wet his pants. He may show jealousy by wanting to sleep with his mother. He may tease the baby or hide his toys. This kind of behavior on the part of the first child has driven many a mother to despair. However, there are several things she can do.

(1.) *Before the baby comes, the mother can prepare the first child for his coming.* She can assure him that there will never be another like him, that he will always be the first, and that there is always a special place in the heart of Mother and Father for the first child. She can remind him that she needs his help in rearing the new baby. She can give him chores to perform. It is also wise for the mother to spend a little less time with the first child during the months of pregnancy which will enable her to build up gradually toward the inevitable.

(2.) *Once the baby has arrived, let the first child stay up 30 minutes or an hour longer than the baby.* Let that be cuddling time and loving time for him. Let it be time that is strictly his.

(3.) *Remind the older child of all the things that he gets and of the unique attention he gets that the baby does not get.* Ride the bicycle around the block with him, and while you are doing it, remind him that you do not do this with the baby. Remind him the baby does not get these privileges.

(4.) *Brag on him when he treats the baby properly.* Let him know how proud you are. Tell him there are children who do not do that, and that you are so proud of him because he loves the new baby. Tell him that it makes you love him even more.

(5.) *Have scheduled times when the two children play with each other.* Do not let them play for too long a period of time, or they will get bored and the rivalry will increase. Let them play at regular intervals by schedule for just enough time before the enjoyment wears off.

(6.) *Be understanding and patient.* Realize that the rivalry and jealousy will come, but the intensity of such rivalry will decline as Mother exercises patience and understanding.

(7.) *The father can help here in the early days by giving extra time to the older child.* Father and child can really become better acquainted as he explains that Mother wants to be with the older child very much, but she has to be with the baby. The dad can explain to the older child how happy he is because this gives him an opportunity to spend more time with him. Their becoming buddies can help alleviate the jealousy and rivalry that is so natural.

(8.) *Much care should be taken to see that the general home atmosphere is happier now that the baby is here.* If it can be obvious to the older child that there is a happier atmosphere at home and that in general everything is better, he will be more apt to accept his new baby brother or baby sister. Some parents have helped solve this problem by gradually lessening the attention given to the first child as the time approaches for the baby's arrival. In other words, gradually less and less time was spent and even a little less affection was given. Then upon the arrival of the baby, they returned to the old expressions and even sweeter ones, thereby enabling the older child to feel that the coming of the baby gave him more attention and more affection from his parents than ever. Subconsciously he could associate this increase with the baby's arrival. He then feels that the baby's coming is better for him than it would have been had there not been an addition to the family.

Regardless of how severe the problem, it must be accepted by the parents as normal, and they must be very patient. The husband must realize how he would feel if another husband came into the home. The wife must realize how she would feel if another wife came into the home. In a sense, this is the way the child feels, for another child has come into the home. Forebearance, patience, understanding, gentleness, longsuffering, kindness and calmness are in order during these important days of adjustment for the young family.

2. *The hospital should be carefully chosen.* The baby's first days of life are in the hospital. They are very important ones. We do not know just how important they are nor what impressions are made in the life of a newborn, but I am convinced that early impressions are important ones. Every effort should be made to give the child an excellent beginning in life.

Talk with your doctor about the hospital. Many people do not realize that there is a direct relationship between the doctor and the hospital. Each doctor uses certain hospitals. The parent has a perfect right to know what will happen and what privileges he will receive at the hospital. He should know their procedures. One new mother said to me, "I wish I had known in advance what I found out when I got to the hospital; I would have gone somewhere else." Another said, "If I had known my doctor works with that particular hospital, I would have chosen another doctor."

The prospective parents should choose a hospital where the father is allowed in the labor room. Some may even want the father to be present in the delivery room, though I do not think this is nearly as important as is his presence in the labor room.

They should choose a hospital that will allow some time for Mother and Father and baby to be together alone so they can get to know each other. Some hospitals allow the mother to keep her baby in her room so they may establish an exact feeding schedule and get to know each other better. It should be a requirement by the mother that the baby be brought to her room to spend some time with her. Bear in mind, as soon as Mother gets home, she will not have all the help she has in the hospital. As much time as possible should be spent with the baby while at the hospital so that the baby may learn to feel instinctively close to Mother and to feel loved by the mother. This also helps the mother to gain confidence in the hospital so that she can feel a certain ease in handling the baby when she gets home. Then she can be fortified with enough experience to care for the baby and not feel helpless when she and the baby are at home together.

It is tragic how impersonal some doctors and hospitals make this sweet personal time of life. The mother should not be insulted by the doctor when she asks for his hospital affiliation. The prospective parent has every right in the world to receive information and make a wise choice. The mother should not be made to feel neurotic and should not be insulted when she asks questions that are legitimate. The hospital staff should not accuse the mother of being overly anxious or untrustful. If there is ever a time when a human being needs compassion and human understanding, it is while at the hospital giving birth to a baby and when learning to know him and love him.

"Rooming-in" probably should not be a prerequisite. The mother should, if offered the choice, arrange to care for the baby in the hospital. Some hospitals provide "rooming-in" facilities. This simply means that the mother may have her baby spend much or even most of his time in her room. The more time the mother can spend with the baby, the better. It is better for the mother and for the baby as well. The more handling, cuddling and contact with the baby that the mother can have the better. It gives the mother a sense of importance, confidence and security. Some hospitals allow the mother to have the baby in her room 24 hours a day. Other hospitals permit the mother to have the baby all day but not all night.

Of course, it is always best for the baby to be placed in the nursery during visiting hours. Since the nursery is usually a glass-enclosed room, visitors can see the baby but cannot transmit infections.

What I am saying is that the mother should be allowed to see the baby often and for lengthy periods, and the mother should take advantage of every opportunity. Mothers make a mistake when they take a vacation while they are in the hospital and see the baby as little as possible. This is especially unwise when it is the first child, for the mother needs all the confidence she can gain while she is in the hospital.

3. *The father should get to know the baby while at the hospital.* The more contact the father has with his baby during the hospital stay, the easier it will be to become adjusted when the baby arrives home. The father should hold the baby when he visits Mother and baby in the hospital. It is also a good idea for him to learn to burp the baby. The baby should, while in the hospital, get to know his father, and the father should get to know the baby. Infants can feel unrest and insecurity, and if they are required to go from the secure hands of the hospital nurse to the insecure hands of Mother and Father, damage could follow. Hence, the father as well as the mother should learn as much of the art of child rearing while at the hospital as possible.

4. *If the hospital allows, the older child or children at home should be allowed to visit Mother and to see the baby while in the hospital.* How sad it is to see a mother in a hospital bed looking out the window waving at some children who are going through one of the most traumatic experiences of their lives! Mother wants to be close to the older children, and they are in desperate need to be close to Mother. The children have a new brother or sister but are unable to see him. They are already jealous and lonesome, and now they are unable to see Mother. Some hospitals wisely allow a certain time when older brothers and sisters can visit Mother and take a glance through the nursery window at baby brother or sister. This should not be a requirement of the hospital chosen by the parents, but if it is allowed, it is a delightful bonus.

5. *Visitors should be as cheerful as possible when visiting the new mother.* They should refrain from giving Mother advice about how to care for the baby. They should not cause any alarm about how the baby looks. They should be very cheerful and optimistic. So often guests will try to persuade Mother not to care for the baby herself when she arrives home. They will tell old wives' tales, elaborate at length on folk medicine, and in general, try to educate the new mother concerning what she ought to do.

If, however, these mistakes are made by visiting friends and relatives, the new mother should smile sweetly, thank them for their advice, and after they are gone, erase it from her mind.

Some of the advice given to new parents is absolutely absurd. I am amazed at how many foolish bits of advice seemingly intelligent and often so-called intellectual people give. For example, the mother is lying in bed with her new baby, the baby's eyes are focused on Mother's face, and the mother says, "Look, my baby is looking at me!" Some well-meaning but foolish self-styled advisor says, "That isn't possible! Your baby can't see yet!"

Now who said the baby can't see yet? Has any baby ever told us that he can't see yet? This is absurd! I am convinced that a newborn can see and does look at his mother's face. Not only is he eating from his mother's body, but he is associating a loving face with that meal. How sweet this is! The sweetest experience that he has learned in life is immediately associated with the sweetest person he will ever know in life. Of course, he *is* looking at his mother! Of this I am convinced.

Another well-meaning expert says, "Well, maybe he can see, but he can only see light and dark or shapes and shadows," and the saddened mother accepts this as fact that her baby cannot see her. This is foolishness. The baby can and does see his mother.

Lying there with that little immortal soul dwelling in a cute precious body, the mother turns to the father and says, "She's looking at me." Then the baby looks toward the father and smiles. The father turns to the doctor or some visitors and says, "Look, the baby is smiling at me." The self-styled experts reply with a statement something like this: "The baby isn't smiling; he has gas on his stomach."

Now I'm not a medical doctor, and I'm not a scientist, but I do know that stomach gas doesn't make you smile. Gas doesn't make an adult smile; why should it make an infant smile! The truth is, it doesn't! It may be that some child will do both at the same time, but a smile is a smile, and I think that the newborn is smiling—smiling because it is happy, content, and because instinctively it knows that it is loved.

There are many other foolish statements that we make at the bedside. It is wise for those of us who visit to limit our remarks to positive ones and not those that will infringe upon the joy of happy people.

6. *The mother should call home to talk to the other child or children several times a day.* She should elaborate as to how much she misses them and how she longs to see them. She should assure them that she is well and that though the baby is cute, it will in no way take the place in her heart of those at home.

The mother could even send a little gift or telegram to the ones at home to assure them. She should pray for them and spend some time consciously loving them while she is in the hospital. She should miss them on purpose so that she will of necessity be so happy to see them when she arrives home.

7. *Mother and Dad must be especially loving to each other during the hospital days.* It is not at all difficult for a child to come between parents. This is tragic. Bear in mind, a potential threat has arrived. The wise husband and wife will give to each other even more attention than ever during these days of adjustment. Special courtesies could be done. The mother, for example, could turn the tables and send the dad a bouquet of flowers at home. She could wire him a box of candy, or before she goes to the hospital, purchase a shirt and tie or some other appropriate gift for him. Have it gift wrapped and hidden. Then while in the hospital she can call him and tell him to look in a certain place and get something for her. Here he will find a delightful surprise! Mother could call Dad at work,

or Dad can call Mother from work. This is so important, for not only will this give assurance to each other, but it can also prepare both of them for the immediate confusion that will arise when returning home.

8. *The hospital time would be a time when the young mother learns to appreciate her own mother and father.* She should not forget them. A special phone call to her dad would be in order. A nice letter written from the hospital bed to her mother would be sweet. The new mother must learn to appreciate more her own mother and to realize the suffering her mother endured bringing her into the world. Then too the grandparents of the new baby are often overlooked. What a nice gesture it would be for them to feel especially loved by a grateful daughter!

9. *The new mother will have some time, perhaps a little more than usual, to pray and to ask God for His blessings on the new baby and the rearranged home.* Vows should be made. Supplication should be offered, and a sweeter relationship with Christ should be enjoyed. Also, the mother could make a schedule of things that she is going to do in training her baby to be all that God wants him to be.

10. *The hospital stay could be a time of reading the Word of God.* During the pregnancy, the mother could use a concordance to find all the Scriptures in the Bible about rearing children. She could read these while in the hospital. She should read at least once through the entire book of Proverbs while in the hospital and vow to God that she is going to do what she can to teach these truths to her child.

11. *The hospital stay should be a time of reading at least one book on child rearing.* Find a book on how to rear children and take it with you to the hos-

pital. Have it packed in your suitcase before you go. (Also, have the Bible packed.) This book on rearing children should be read carefully while the mother is in the hospital.

12. *The entire family should come to the hospital to get Mother and baby.* The children should greet her. The moment Mother gets in the car, she should assure the older child or children of her love and of how much she has missed them and how proud of them she is.

13. *Dad and the children should have a nice "Welcome home!" celebration prepared for Mother.* This should not be too exciting or exhausting. Maybe a big sign could be placed in the front yard. Perhaps a beautiful bouquet of flowers and a "welcome home" note from each member of the family could be at the bedside. Maybe a tape could be made by each child and the father so that Mother can play the tape while resting after returning home and realize how much she was missed and how much she is loved. Maybe Mother's favorite meal could be ready for her. Perhaps gifts could be waiting for her upon her arrival. Everything possible should be done by Dad and the older children to make Mother feel welcome. Also, everything possible should be done by Mother to let the rest of the family know that the new member of the home will never in any way take the place in her heart of those that God previously has given to her.

Chapter Three

NOW YOU ARE AT HOME!

There are few days in the life of a family that can compare with the day that baby comes home from the hospital, and yet often that day becomes a day of disappointment because the new mother and father had so many wonderful plans. They had planned to sit down and have a dedication service, but baby wan't in the mood to be reverent. They had planned to sit down and read the Bible together, but baby wasn't very spiritual. Now they are home only to find that it is not what they had thought it would be.

In the hospital Mother spent a lot of time getting organized. She had planned exactly what she was going to do, and in her opinion, she was going to be a tremendous success. Things, however, didn't quite work out that way. Mother soon finds that having a baby at home requires a lot of altered plans and flexibility. In fact, oftentimes it makes parents feel that perhaps it wasn't worth it. Most of us just do not know what having a baby at home would be like. Some might even think that if they had known what it was like, they would not have wanted to have children at all. Sleep, peace, organization and quiet are at a premium, and the sweet, precious plans that have been made for nine months vanish with the colic.

If a couple will realize before the baby comes that it will be hectic for awhile, everything will go better. Babies do wake up at night; many babies wake up many times through the night; some babies wake up four, five, six times a night. Maybe these suggestions will help:

1. *Both parents should help with the baby through the night.* Someone will say, "Well, the father has to work, and because he has a job and the mother is at home where she can sleep some, she should take care of the baby through the night." Someone else will say, "The father should do it because the baby needs a mother who is rested, not one who is haggered, tired and impatient." Now a happy solution to this problem is to have the parents take shifts. One parent could take from 9:00 p.m. to 3:00 a.m.; and the other, from 3:00 a.m. to 9:00; or one parent could take from 9:00 p.m. to 1:30 a.m. and the other, from 1:30 a.m. to 6:00 a.m. This insures each parent some sleep that is uninterrupted, and perhaps during the rest of the night, he will get a little bit of sleep.

2. *Do not have the baby in the room with you, Mother and Father.* Protect your privacy! Of course, it will require you to walk a longer distance to get to the baby, but it will give you time alone together, and your privacy is protected. This is so important!

This is also not good for the older child. If Mom, Dad and baby are together in one room and the older child is in another, this causes the child to think that the baby is getting preferential treatment, and he will feel like an outcast, exiled to his own room.

3. *It is also wise not to put the new baby in the same room with the older child.* Let the baby have his own room, if possible. If, for example, there is a three-bedroom house, Mom and Dad can have one bedroom; the older child, another; and the baby, another. If there must be some doubling up because of older children, let the older children sleep in the same room, and let the baby have a

room of his own. Older children like their privacy. They feel it has been infringed upon if the baby moves into their room. This concern causes him to be overly protective of his own toys, his own bed, and his own private things. Have the older child or children sleep under the new arrangements several weeks before the baby comes. The older child will not associate his new sleeping arrangements with the baby's coming.

4. *It is best for the new baby to have his own crib.* I would not suggest that the same crib be used for each child. It could place in the mind of the older child the thought that someone has taken his place. It might even be wise to put the crib of the older child somewhere in a very special place leaving it empty so that he can see that his crib is still his. If for any reason the older crib must be used, it should be repainted or redecorated so that it will not look the same.

5. *Plan visiting hours.* Visitors can rudely interrupt well made plans. A good way to prevent this is for the new parents to predict the most likely visitors and to call them upon returning home from the hospital, inviting them to come at a certain time. The mother might call her closest friend and say, "Mary, I'm home from the hospital, and I can't wait to see you. Could you come by tomorrow afternoon about 2:00?" An appointment can be made, and this will become a part of the schedule for the parents.

6. *The parents should have time alone for privacy and intimacy with each other.* When a child comes, Mom and Dad will have to fight for such time. It may be that they will seldom sit down to dinner together. Before the baby came, they ate alone. Now it's hard to eat at all. Before the baby came, the meals were prepared. After the baby

comes, the husband often eats leftovers. The mother is tired; the father needs attention. Before you know it, both will think the other is being selfish. Bitterness can develop toward the innocent child who has placed a wedge between them. If such resentment builds up, the husband and wife should discuss it openly before it becomes serious. The truth is that neither the husband or the wife knows how the other is going to react after the baby comes. It is a stimulus that they have not faced. They must have privacy with each other. It must be remembered that in a few years that baby's crib will become a honeymoon suite and that an older and wiser couple will say, "Goodbye," to their offspring. How important it is that they cultivate their relationship and see to it that this newborn cements their relationship and makes it deeper and sweeter!

Chapter Four

TEACHING CHARACTER

Someone has said that character is the subconscious doing of right. It is when right and the doing of right becomes a reflex. This can happen only by continued practice of doing right in response to certain stimuli. Basically, it is the forming of proper habits. Naturally, the earlier these habits are formed and the earlier the doing of right becomes a matter of reflex and enters into the subconscious, the stronger will be the character of the adult. Hence, proper habits should be started at birth.

1. *Proper eating habits.* Babies are people, and all people enjoy eating. We learn very early in life that eating brings us pleasure and delight. This pleasure is caused not only because eating brings relief from hunger, but also because of the by-products that eating brings. In the infant, for example, eating will bring the joy of being close to Mother, the warmth of the mother's breast, the feeling of being loved and cared for, and the joy of being held and rocked. As the baby grows older, there are other extras he receives from eating. Because of this, it is very important that proper eating habits are developed so that the child can derive these pleasures from the eating of good, nourishing food along with other proper eating habits.

The first development of proper eating habits is the first nursing from his mother's breast. The baby will no doubt be hungry and perhaps will be crying. Hence, the first nursing should be a happening. The baby will at least by instinct enjoy such a feeding. Let him snuggle for awhile; do not hurry him, and when he is ready he will begin to eat. Let him hear soft words. Commune from your heart to his. Sing gently to him, and let his first association with nourishing eating be that of many other pleasantries. At each nursing that follows, make it a real happening for the child. Then as he grows older, is weaned, and settles down to a child's diet, continue making mealtime one of the most delightful of the day.

Remember, taste is cultivated. The reason that our generation loves junk food instead of good, nourishing food is that we have cultivated a taste for food that is less healthful. During infancy is the time when children should be led to develop a spiritual appetite. A child can learn to like nuts more than he likes junk snacks if his taste is so trained. He can learn to like fruit more than he likes candy if he is trained properly. Good vegetables can appeal to him as much or more than excessive starches if he is led to develop the proper eating habits from infancy.

The child should also be trained to eat on schedule. One of the great secrets of life is to live by schedule, and the healthy person is one who eats by schedule. A good little slogan for the feeding of an infant, and for that matter for the feeding of people at any age would be, "Eat the proper food at the proper time in the proper environment.

2. *Sleep habits.* Sleep habits are developed just like eating habits and should be established in early infancy. These habits, like eating habits, will only be developed and maintained if pleasure is derived. Hence, the wise parents will make the sleep time as pleasant as possible. Sleep habits, like eating habits, should be on schedule. A very young baby will probably sleep 18-20 hours out of the 24. This need for sleep gradually diminishes until a six-

month-old baby is likely to sleep 14-15 hours of the 24. During the first year of life, most babies require one long nap during the day and one short one. At 12-15 months of age the child usually gives up the short one and has one long nap a day plus the night sleep. The number of hours a child sleeps or the number of hours of sleep he requires is not as important as the fact that his sleep is regularly scheduled. The child is learning in infancy to live by discipline and by schedule. The child should go to bed the same time every night, get up at the same time every morning and take his daily naps at the same time, and the naps should be for the same length of time. Many mothers could have avoided nervous problems in their own systems had they worked a little harder at first in securing the baby's schedule.

Now, let us get back to the happening of sleep. A child should learn to associate sleep with being comfortable, being at the right temperature, being changed, being loved and being fed. If extra affection and attention can be given at sleep time, then the sleep time can become one of the highlights of the day for the child. He soon develops a positive association with sleep. This is vital.

Several things should be avoided in making the child's sleep habits desirable.

(1.) Do not let the baby get into the habit of going to sleep with a bottle. Under such circumstances neither eating or sleeping is as pleasant as it should be.

(2.) Do not let the baby sleep alone in the house. In fact, an infant should not be left alone in the house at any time, even if he is sound asleep.

Once the baby has gone to sleep, do not wake him up. Oh, yes, friends will come in to see him; let them see him asleep. Do not wake him up to show him off after he has gone to sleep.

After dark, do not take the baby out for too much excitement. Taking him to the church nursery is certainly proper, but too much noise and too many bright lights before bedtime will cause him to be restless.

By all means, do not give the baby any kind of medicine to make him sleep unless it is done with doctor's orders.

There is so much in the subconscious and in the instincts that it is very important not only to let a baby have a daily schedule but also a weekly schedule. He can look forward to the nursery on Sunday and on Wednesday night and to other pleasant activities that are regularly scheduled each week.

Few of us as adults know our own bodies. Few of us know how much sleep our bodies need. Much of this is due to the fact that from infancy we have led undisciplined, unscheduled lives and among these undisciplined activities are our sleeping habits.

3. *Toilet training.* Every young mother anticipates the day when her baby can stay clean and dry. Because of this, many begin this training too early. A baby is nearly a year old before his nervous system is developed enough to warrant the beginning of toilet training. At this time, the child usually is becoming aware when you praise him for doing well. It is then time to begin serious toilet training. Subject to schedule and discipline, the child should be put on the toilet at certain regular times. These times should be when he wakes up in the morning, at the conclusion of each meal, before he takes a nap, when he wakes from his nap, etc. If the mother will keep a record for a week or two of the hours the baby is wet or has had a bowel movement, it will help her in planning a schedule so as to anticipate his needs. Do not use the scolding

method. Do not be negative. Do not spank him. Rather, use the praise incentive. Let him associate proper elimination with Mother's pleasure and praise. Be patient with him; it will take time and understanding.

Keep the baby in diapers until he learns to walk, and then replace them with pants. This will help him get the idea there is a change in his elimination habits. By the way, do not leave the child wet. If he has an accident, go ahead and change him. Do not scold him. When he does wait until potty time, give him such praise that he will want to earn this praise again.

4. *Thumb sucking.* Sucking is natural with a child. He began his life by getting his food that way, and since he is a born explorer, he usually puts an object to his mouth quickly after birth. Thumb sucking is a prevalent problem for babies. It usually becomes intense somewhere around 6 months of age. Occasionally the baby also finds that he can suck his fingers. Usually he will overcome his habit if the parents do not make too much fuss over it. It is never wise to punish for this. It is often wise to use a toy or other attention-getters with which to divert the attention of the baby from his sucking.

Thumb sucking becomes a problem usually while the baby is being weaned. Since babies are born with a tremendous instinct to suck, even apart from the instinct of hunger, it is often difficult to cure him quickly from his sucking desire. Hence, when the cup takes the place of the bottle or the breast, the most convenient thing for the baby to do is suck his thumb.

A mother came to me and told me that her 3-year-old son was still sucking his thumb. She told me she had done everything she could do to stop him. I asked her what she had tried. She said she had tried to make the boy ashamed. She had made such statements as, "I'm ashamed of you, and your daddy is ashamed of you." She then told me she had ridiculed him, calling him a "little bitty baby." Then she tried the tactic of the fear of father: "I'm going to tell your daddy when he comes home! What will he think?" Then she had tried spanking the thumb after she had worked it out of his mouth. At night she had tied his thumbs in mittens. There are other things she had tried which she included in her statement of, "I have tried everything!" I reminded her that thumb sucking itself was not nearly as dangerous as the improper handling of the situation by the parents and that the most dangerous thing about the child's thumb sucking was the action that it had prompted the parents to take.

Then the mother told me of the fears she had concerning her son's thumb sucking. She was afraid of a permanent injury to the thumb. She was afraid that it would spoil the shape of his teeth and his jaw. She was afraid that it would cause the child to be withdrawn and introverted and, of course, she was afraid that it would go on and on and on into his school days. Now in rare cases, such damage is possible, but in more cases, the damage is done by the parents' overreaction.

The matter that should occupy our time is that of learning WHY the child sucks his thumb. There are many reasons. The thumb becomes a comfort to the child. He turns to thumb sucking when he wants comforting or when he feels he is not loved enough or safe enough or not good enough. The thumb comforts and assures him. The wise parent will realize this and will give the child sufficient comfort, assurance, self-confidence, self-esteem, etc. Again, the positive approach is the best one.

When you see the child not sucking his thumb, brag on him, make him feel like he has done something great. Reward him for it with the feeling of satisfaction and accomplishment. What the child has been doing subconsciously is telling you that he is not completely satisfied with everything about life. There is something missing which he needs. Asking, pleading and scolding will not solve his problem, for it is not his problem. Putting pressure on it only adds to his need and to the frame of mind which caused the thumb sucking in the first place. Hence, the parents' efforts prolong the habit.

Some feel that if a child is allowed to suck his thumb all he chooses, he will relinquish his thumb sucking sooner than if he is urged to stop it. Let the parent be comforted in the fact that most children give up their thumb sucking shortly after they enroll in school. When they come in contact with other children, pride develops and the child is embarrassed to have his peers see him with such an infantile habit. The wise parent will not try to stop the thumb sucking but will rather try to stop the causes for the thumb sucking. Remember that alarm and force will lengthen rather than abbreviate the longevity of this habit. Do not punish. Do not remind him constantly. Do not threaten him that he will injure his fingers or buck his teeth. Do not remind him that if he loves you, he would stop sucking his thumb. Do not use such phrases as, "You are a big boy now!" "Aren't you ashamed of yourself!" "You are such a baby!" Do not wrap his hands or use mittens. Do not use elbow splints or anything to keep his arm from bending. Do not use sleeping garments which hold his arms down. Do not put bitter, disagreeable, distasteful substances on his fingers. Let him know that you love him so much and are so proud of him that he will have so much assurance and security that he will not need his thumb. Have him trade the comfort of his thumb for the comfort of a secure relationship with Mom and Dad. By all means, do not panic.

There are some things that can be done. Let the child suck longer when he eats. Let him nurse as long as he wishes. If he is bottle fed, get another nipple with a smaller hole so that it will take him longer to drink his milk. As he grows older, don't let him get bored. Be sure he has enough toys, enough things to stimulate his mind and to attract his attention. Also notice when he sucks. Does he suck when he is lonely? Does he suck when he is frightened? Does he suck when he feels deserted? Once you have found the cause, then you can satisfy his need and over a period of time eliminate the thumb sucking altogether.

As he gets older, see if you think he gets too much or too little attention, has too many or too few companions, is mothered too much or too little, gets more or less attention than the other children. Take an intelligent survey and set up a diligent plan to eliminate excesses and fill voids.

5. *Bed wetting.* By the time the average child reaches the age of 2, he can stay dry during the daytime. However, it is usually a year or more before he can stay dry while asleep. The average child is able to stay dry during the nighttime by the time he is 3, but not all children are average. Approximately 25% of all children wet the bed after the age of 7. It is thought by some that boys have some more difficulty in bed wetting than girls. It is comforting to know that usually this problem is hereditary and that the parent of such a child had the same problem when he was a child.

Because the problem is such a messy one, parents become excessively alarmed and overreact in an effort to execute its cure. It may be true that early training in an effort to correct bed wetting may actually be the cause of bed wetting later on. Take it easy; don't rush; a few extra months of diaper washing when a child is one or two may save months of panty and sheet washing two or three years later. Accept the fact that children differ in this as they do in other things. Some achieve success many months before others. Keep in mind the following things when wetting is a problem.

(1.) *Do not ridicule or give the child the idea that you would love him more if he would stop wetting.*

(2.) *Do not show annoyance.* Try not even to feel annoyed. The child needs your help. No doubt he is nervous and insecure. He does not need to feel your nervousness or insecurity.

(3.) *Try to be casual.* Build his confidence. Assure him that he will do better someday. Give him extra affection. Praise him more than usual. Brag on him when he does well. Brag on other things he does perhaps better than other children. Do not make him feel inferior. You will help him a lot more by leaving him to be relaxed than making him tense because he feels he is a failure.

(4.) *Do not give him prizes for being dry.* Give him praise and love at all times but especially when he does well.

(5.) *Do not make a big deal of toilet training.* By all means, don't use threats, shaming, rewards, punishment as methods with which to train your child.

If you will follow these suggestions, you are not going to make the child dry right away, but you will make him happier, you will make him more relaxed, you will make him more of an extrovert, and you will give him more security. A secure, confident, happy child will achieve dryness much earlier than one who is made tense and high-strung by overly anxious parents.

If the child who has become dry has an accident, treat it casually. Do not scold. Follow the advice given concerning thumb sucking. Do not be as concerned about the act itself as by the cause of the act. Correct the causes; fill the voids; stop the excesses; give security, love and praise, and unless there is a medical reason (and there usually is not) the problem will be solved in due time. By all means, be patient. The child is like you. His troubles pile up on him. Too much is expected from him and he becomes frustrated. This is when things fall apart. Bear in mind that his problems are as serious to him as yours are to you. Calm, rational, tender treatment will win out in the long run.

A number of things could cause his insecurities. Something in his life could be troubling him, making him tense and anxious. Perhaps he is not on schedule in other activities of his life. Maybe his parents create tension in the home. Maybe the child lacks self-confidence. Maybe he has an inferiority complex because of older brothers and sisters. Maybe he does not feel approved. Maybe he does not feel he excels in any area.

Of course, there are a few things that can be done. Some parents take the child to the bathroom when they retire. This often enables the child to go through the night dry. The best thing to do is take it in stride, not make an issue of it, and soon the problem will solve itself.

6. *Fingernail biting.* Children have many nervous habits. Many of these are typical such as blinking the eyes, picking the nose and, the most common of all, fingernail biting. It must be understood that children are perpetual motion. Freedom of movement is necessary part of their development. To tell

a child to sit still is asking for a miracle. Hence, if a child is forced to be still for a long period of time and if he is asked to keep from talking, he becomes fidgety. Habits like nail biting soon develop. If you will notice carefully, nail biting usually occurs when the child is repressed or is unduly excited or unhappy. There are several sets of circumstances that usually increase nail biting. Anything that causes the child inner tension such as fear or worry make conditions right for the habit. A nervous mother, an anxious parent, or quarreling in the home can upset a child and lead him to nail biting. If too much is expected of him, he may turn to his fingernails. The wise parent should watch the child to see when he bites his nails and then seek a trend. Parents will notice there are certain things, times or experiences that prompt the biting of the nails. After such a study has been made, the parent can eliminate the conditions that warrant the nail biting.

There are several things that can be done after the cause of the strain has been eliminated. The child can be given something to do with his hands that will keep him busy. The child's nails should be kept in good condition. They should be short and smooth with no hang nails, which will help remove the temptation to bite them. It is not a good idea to put bitter tasting substances on the nails. However, sometimes some clear nail polish on a little girl's nails will give her pride in them and often eliminate the nail biting.

The biting of the nails is another one of those nervous habits which are likely to develop when a child is not serene and happy, whose routine is not planned and who is put under strain, giving him too much with which to cope. Sometimes having to play with older children can stimulate nail biting.

Living in an unhappy home where there is fussing can have the same result. If a child is not allowed to play outdoors enough, it can drive him to this habit. One thing that must be remembered is that children are often too overprotected, over-mothered and over-managed. Once again, assurance, love and security can go a long way toward correcting the biting of the nails. Do not resort to scolding and threats. Do not make constant mention of the biting; that will only make it worse. Nail biting, like bed wetting and thumb sucking, is best corrected by a quiet study of the conditions surrounding the habit and then eliminating them. Once again, the wise parent should not make a big issue over it, for big issues are causes, not cures.

Try bragging on the child when he does well. Tell him how pretty his fingernails are when he does not bite them, but even then, a calm type of complimenting should be carried out. Do not panic. Set out to provide a serene, assuring, securing atmosphere by eliminating boredom, tense or overly emotional radio and television programs, insecurities, etc.

7. *Temper tantrums.* You will find excellent cooperation in a normal baby. However, when the baby is becoming a child and is walking and talking, probably in the late part of his second year or the early part of his third year, some changes take place. He suddenly has a tremendous desire to assert himself and to be heard! This assertion may show itself in temper tantrums. What is happening is that the child is becoming a human being. He is walking and talking now, and he suddenly has a desire to make some of his own decisions. He expresses this desire with temper tantrums. He decides that he is restricted too much. He may decide not to dress when you want to dress him or

he may choose not to give up some object that you want him to surrender to you. He may decide he doesn't want to eat, and if he does eat, he doesn't want to eat what you want him to eat. He wants to do things by himself. Now there are several things that can be done.

(1.) *The parent must set a good example by having an even disposition.* You yourself must not have a "short fuse." If the child sees you losing your temper, he will soon decide that is the way to express one's self when he is not pleased. On the other hand, if the child sees the parent manifesting behavior that is calm and quiet, he is more likely to perform in the same manner. Avoid having a nervous, loud environment, for the child will eventually pattern his behavior after that of his parents and his home atmosphere. If you do not control your temper, he will not control his. If you are loud and angry when you do not have your way, he will be loud and angry when he does not have his way.

(2.) *Do not let your child's temper tantrums cause you to lose your temper.* Never reward his tantrums. If a child cries to get something, never give it to him. Let him know that the way to get what he wants is by behaving properly, not be exposing his temper. Never, never, never reward him for his temper tantrum. Many parents become so exasperated by the child's behavior they attempt to bribe him to be good by giving him what he wants or what he would enjoy. This is a tragic mistake. Reward goodness, not badness. Reward a pleasant personality and disposition, not an unpleasant one.

(3.) *Build such a close relationship with the child that the breaking of fellowship with the parents will be the worst punishment possible.* The worst thing about a punishment and the worst punishment should be the fact that fellowship is broken between the child and parent. When there is a relationship that is sweet and enjoyed by both, the child does not want to have that relationship broken. Hence, the parent can simply ignore the child when he is having a temper tantrum (that is, if the tantrum is not caused by some health problem or severe discomfort). Make the child realize that fellowship with the parent is good when he is quiet and bad when he is throwing a temper tantrum. It is often good to let the child cry it out. In the case of a baby, the parent should see if the diaper is dry. He should be sure no pins are sticking the child's body. He should convince himself that the child is not crying excessively because he is ill. He should be sure the child is not crying because he is hungry or covered too tightly. He should be sure the child is not crying because of a stomach ache. Once he is convinced these things are all in order, he should then let the child cry. Simply close the door to his room, go in the other room and be about your responsibilities. When he does stop his crying and is quiet for a few minutes, go to his room and brag on him for being quiet. Let him realize that the fellowship is restored when he does not cry and that it is broken when he does cry. Do not let him think the way to get picked up and be babied is to scream. It is better to prevent the temper tantrums than to cure them.

It is wise, as has been stated previously, for a child to live by schedule, thereby developing lifetime habits. It will help his disposition tremendously if he is getting enough sleep and sleeping on schedule, if he is having his meals on time and is living a scheduled, disciplined life. Sometimes the parent spends too much time with the child. This time should also be scheduled time. A child should learn to be alone. He should learn to enjoy being alone. It will give him security and assurance for the rest of his life. Suppose, for example, that he wakes up around 7:00 in the morning. His mother gives him some words of assurance, a hug and a kiss, feeds him, bathes him, changes his clothes and puts him back to bed. He should be taught to spend some time alone then. Perhaps at mid-morning the mother could come in at a scheduled time, take the child up and spend 30 minutes playing with him and loving him. The child could then be put back to bed to spend some more time alone. Soon comes lunch time. After lunch the child can be changed and put to bed for his afternoon nap. After his nap Mother can take 30 minutes more and play with him and love him. Then he should be put back to bed or in his playpen or in his room if there is an accordion door to keep him from escaping, where he can spend some more time alone before Daddy comes home. This means that Mother has not only spent some time bathing and feeding him, but she has spent 30 minutes in the morning and 30 minutes in the afternoon playing with him and loving him. It is my feeling that many children go bad because their parents spend too much time with them. It is not how much time a parent spends but what kind of time he spends. A child needs to feel the security of genuine love and interest from his parents and the security of the enjoyment of being alone. Both are important.

Many parents spend much time with all their children and little or no time alone with each child. I think it is best for there to be a scheduled time for each child. The child thereby gets to know his parent on personal basis. He does not feel like one of a group but one that is very special. This not only enables the child to know the parent better but it enables the parent to know each child as an individual. This does not have to be a lot of time. When our children were small I would take them on dates. For example, I would take one of the girls up to the shopping center. Then I would purchase for her whatever her need was at the time—a dress, a pair of shoes or some underclothing. Sometimes I would even buy her a little toy. Then we would go to the park to swing. An hour is a long time to a child. It does not seem very long to an adult, but when a parent spends an hour alone with a child, it seems to him a very long time. This planned fellowship should start in infancy.

A planned time when the child is alone should also start in infancy. He should get to know himself. When our children were small, I would go outside and the child and I would sit on a quilt in the front yard together. I would then, after awhile, tiptoe into the house and watch him through the window. I would let him play alone for awhile. This would help teach him not to be afraid of being alone. He also needs to learn not to be afraid of the dark. Both are lessons a child needs to learn early in life.

It is usually best not to spank the child for throwing a temper tantrum. Brief isolation would be better. Especially is this a tremendous form of punishment when the child is close to his parent. A spanking would be more in order if there is direct disobedience. I am not saying that spanking is wrong. Quite to the contrary, spanking is right, and we are admonished in the Scriptures to do so, but during these early days of life, a child is using a temper tantrum to get what he wants. He wants Mom to pick him up; he wants attention. If he learns that he does not get the attention by crying and exposing his temper, he will soon try other methods. It is the parent's responsibility to let him know what methods will work. When he finds that goodness will work, he will then use goodness to get his desired result. However, if the parents' actions let him know that being bad will work, he will then be bad for the rest of his life to get what he wants.

A generation ago noted child psychologists who knew little about psychology and less about children advanced the theory that the child should not have his progress retarded. "Give him what he wants," they said. "He is only trying to express himself." We gave these children what they wanted because we did not want to impede their progress. That generation is now grown up. They are still getting what they want! They are rioting, demonstrating, burning buildings, destroying property, infringing on the safety of society, and in general, are ruining the greatest country on the face of the earth! They were taught to get what they wanted by bad behavior. We gave it to them then and we are giving it to them now, and the greatest nation on the face of the earth is crumbling before our eyes. If a nation's character is salvaged, we will have to begin where its deterioration began—in the crib. It was in the crib where this generation of lawlessness was spawned. It will be in the crib where another generation of law and order is conceived. Through all of this a child MUST learn to respect his parents. This respect will be caused by a parent being firm but calm, manifesting the spirit of Christ in gentleness yet firmness. A parent who responds by jerking a child or throwing a temper tantrum of his own is joining the child in his crime and mixing wrong with wrong.

(4.) *Brag on the child when he is good.* I remember my mother saying to a neighbor while I was in another room (she made a special point to say it loudly enough so I could hear her), "My Jack is a good boy! I know some boys who are bad boys who scream and cry, but my son is a good boy. I'm so proud of him!" I would hear her from the other room, and my hat size would double as I would hear my mother brag on me to a neighbor. She was setting for me a reputation that I wanted to fulfill. When I did enter the room, I would be the picture of goodness, a model son, for I was trying to live up to my reputation and prove to the neighbor lady that my mother was right. Sometimes my mother would set me on her knee and tell me, "Son, I was in another home the other day, and they had a boy about your age. He was so rowdy and loud we could hardly talk. I am so proud of you because you are such a fine fellow. You are never rowdy and you never interrupt. You never embarrass me when we have company. I'm sure glad that little boy isn't my little boy; I'm glad you are my little boy because you are not like him." Once again she was setting for me an ideal and a reputation that I wanted to uphold. This tactic certainly is far better than a slap across the face or the jerk of the arm or the screaming voice.

8. *Speech defects.* Since speech is the means humans use to communicate one with another, anything that interferes with this type of communication becomes a real handicap. Most speech defects can be cured in the home by the loving help of wise parents. Children begin to use words during their second year. Much care should be taken to help the child speak properly. If a child should go into his third year or even very far beyond his second birthday without developing normal speech, the parents should examine the following possibilities. The child may not need to talk to get what he wants. Perhaps he can grunt and the parent knows what he

wants. Perhaps he can simply make a gesture to receive his desires. The parent should in such cases require the child to speak before he gets what he wants. In other words, the parent should see to it that the child needs to talk. Mother and Dad should lead him to make his wants known by the communication of speech.

Some parents give too much attention to the child's words and speaking. In some cases they even show off the child for visitors, and he may be asked to repeat the same words over and over again. This often leads the child to become embarrassed and in many cases it slows up his speech progress. When this is true, the wise parents will leave the child alone and try not to show him off to guests. When a child does speak, the parent should show definite interest, but not undue excitement.

Sometimes the parents do not talk enough. Many children do not talk because they do not hear enough talking. Read to the child. Talk to him. Let him hear you talk. This will stimulate the child to join you in conversation. The child of a non-talkative parent will usually talk later than children whose parents communicate often with them and read to them.

Sometimes a child may talk for awhile and then slow down his talking. This may be because he has other interests. Perhaps he has found some other avenue of development that temporarily intrigues him more. Maybe he is learning to do something else for the first time, and talking is not new to him any more. In such cases, do not be alarmed; simply keep talking, singing and reading to the child. Keep on loving him. He will return to his vocabulary after he has mastered the thing that is occupying his mind.

An undisciplined life can cause the child to talk

later than normal. So many things depend on
schedule. The child that gets up on time, eats on
time, sleeps on time, is bathed on time, is dressed
on time, is loved on time, etc. will be in general
more normal and more healthy. He will come
nearer talking on time.

Some children talk late because of strife in the
home. If a child hears fussing and screaming, he
will not be interested in developing the art of speaking because the spoken word will become distasteful to him. If, however, kind words are spoken,
and if speech is an expression of love, kindness and
gentleness, the child will be impressed by its use and
will usually want to talk earlier. Of course, there is
always the possibility of some illness which makes
it difficult for the child to talk. If he is nearing his
third birthday and still is not talking much, his
hearing should be tested. He should be given a
thorough check-up and maybe be taken to a neurol-
ogist. Of course, sometimes the child has a speech
impairment due to a harelip or a cleft palate. In this
case he should be taken to a speech therapist for
special training.

There are three times in life when stuttering is a
temptation: (1) When a child is around 2½ years
old and is just beginning to talk freely, (2) When he
enters school, and (3) When he becomes an adolescent. These are times of big adjustments and because of this, stuttering may develop. Speech difficulty is caused by emotional strain and frustration.
When a child is 2 or 3 years of age, he is so desirous
to make himself understood. He is just beginning
to talk freely and does not have a large enough
vocabulary to express his thoughts. He is not able
to put into words what he wants to ask or tell. Because of this bother he sometimes stutters. It is a
good idea not to have him in close contact with an

adult or teenager who stutters. At least such a person should not be a constant companion to the child.

Do not correct or scold the child for stuttering. Repeat or talk more slowly. Do not fuss at him. If he appears to be looking for a word, fill in the extra word for him. Listen to him carefully and patiently. Do not make him feel that he must hurry when he tries to express himself. The stuttering child feels he will not have time to give his expression. Do not tell him he has plenty of time; simply show him by being patient. Rearrange his schedule; keep tension from his life. Lessen the rush-rush atmosphere of the home.

Sometimes the stuttering will take place after he has been playing with several children and has become too excited. If this is the case, let him play with one or two children at a time. In other words, take away from him temptations to nervousness and frustration. Act like nothing is wrong. Take him as he is. Don't lead him to think you wish he would hurry up and say what he is trying to say. Like bed wetting, thumb sucking, nail biting and other nervous expressions, stuttering is usually caused by a home situation that is too tense, too hurried, or where there is too much strife. Its cure comes by eliminating these causes. The parent should not expect miracles. It may take some time. Do not panic. Be calm, loving, patient and understanding. In almost every case in due time victory will come. If the stuttering is not cured when the child is nearing four or five, professional help should be sought.

If a child is left-handed, let him be left-handed. It has been thought by many that there is a connection between left-handedness and stuttering. There are those who believe that when the left-handed child is encouraged to use his right hand, this causes stuttering. This is probably not necessarily true. Rather, the type of parent who would be embarrassed to have a left-handed child and who would attempt to coerse him to use his right hand might be the type of parent who would cause stuttering anyway and to whom a child would usually speak with caution and tension. It would be far better for the parent, with patience, to lead the child to become efficient with his left hand rather than causing him to become nervous by being a less-than-average right-hander.

There are other speech problems besides delayed speech and stuttering. There is the problem of omission of a sound in words. For example, a child may say "pease" for "please," which means he is omitting a certain sound. Then sometimes the child will have an enunciation problem. There is also the problem of careless and inaccurate sounds such as misuse of the letter "s." Sometimes the child will even add unnecessary sounds. Regardless of the problem, unless it is a physical one, the parent should first attempt to have a quiet, peaceful setting in the home. He should be the type of person to whom the child likes to speak. He should not expect the child to act like an adult or speak like an adult. He should avoid undue excitement, hurry and pressure. He should not expect the child to recite too much, and he should not show off the child. In other words, just a normal, kind, peaceful atmosphere in the home and a sweet relaxed atmosphere with the child is the best treatment. Add to this, proper pronunciation by the parents, and you will usually find the answer. This, of course, is the best cure and should be tried at length before consulting professional help.

Chapter Five

SPEND SOME TIME AWAY
FROM YOUR BABY!

You must realize that you can't spend every minute of the day with your baby. Time should be carefully planned where the mother can be away from the baby some. This time should not be for long periods, or the child may begin to fail to respond to the parents. The baby will sense if you like to be with him or not, and he will detach himself from you if you are not careful. In the first year or so of life, even short periods of separation can cause the baby to react negatively and even to ignore the parents after they have been away for two or three days. It is also possible for the child to become attached to the person who cares for the baby and to turn to him for his security and comfort. Because of this, the time away from the baby should be brief and planned as follows:

1. *Have several baby sitters on whom you can call.* Choose baby sitters who like children and enjoy playing with them and who express warmth while they care for your child. Do not choose a baby sitter who is more concerned about neatness than warmth and love. Choose babysitters who will carry out your wishes and instructions to the letter.

2. *When the babysitter comes to the house, have her come a bit early.* Have her there long enough before you leave so the baby will become familiar with the babysitter. I would suggest that the babysitter should arrive at least a half an hour early. This should be done regardless of the age of the child. The babysitter should come while the child is

awake. It is quite a shocking experience for a child to wake up and find a stranger with him. Be sure that the child is awake and that the babysitter spends some time with the child gaining his confidence before you leave. Otherwise, the child may begin to associate sleep with your leaving. This may cause the child to be reluctant to go to sleep for fear you will not be there when he awakens. It is best that your child know that you are leaving and that he be aware of it even if he cries.

3. *Even though you have a list of babysitters, it is best to use the same one as much as possible.* Children do not like strangers. They should not have to associate the arrival of a stranger with Mother's departure. Serious emotional difficulties can arise.

4. *Plan a schedule of time or times that you will be away from the baby.* I would suggest that the parents use a babysitter at least once a week. This would be for going to a restaurant to eat or having some recreational time together. This could be for an evening out or an afternoon and evening out. I would also suggest that at least once every two months the parents take an overnight outing. Perhaps they could go to a motel for the night and then spend the day shopping or participating in some type of recreation. I would not suggest that parents take long vacations away from their infant child. Several brief absences a year would be much better than one lengthy one.

5. *The mother should resume her spiritual activities as soon as possible.* The good Christian mother will want to go soul winning every week as soon as she is strong enough. She will want to particpate in church activities such as missionary societies, class meetings, etc. She will be a better mother if she spends time fulfilling her Christian responsibilities outside the home. Go ahead, Mother, and teach the

Sunday school class. Go ahead and work with the young people. Do not spend your entire life or even a majority of your life doing it, but you do need outside interests.

Use the church nursery. New mother, as soon as you are able to go to church, you should return to the services. You can have some time apart from the baby while you are in the services and the baby is being cared for in the church nursery. Now the nursery may not be as nice as you wish it were, but God is able to care for your baby. I would rather see the baby in a nursery that is not quite the picture of cleanliness than for mother not to receive the spiritual food that she needs. Do not take the child to the services! Babies can disrupt the services and prevent people from coming to Christ. A little baby can also keep the mother from getting what she needs from the services. You need your spiritual food. You need edification that comes from the preaching of the Word of God. Put your baby in the nursery. Trust him to the Lord, and you go to church.

6. *If the mother works, she should try to come home in the middle of the day.* There are cases, of course, when Mother must be away at a secular job. If possible, the mother should cut down on her working hours during the first two years of the child's life. If this is not possible, the mother should try to come home for lunch. I would suggest that the mother try not to be away from the child for more than four hours at a time. If the mother cannot come home during the day, perhaps the father could come home during the day and spend some time with the child.

Now I am not advocating mothers working. I am saying that when mothers have to work they should make every possible effort to be with the child as much as possible. The wise employer should make it possible for parents of children under the age of two to organize their schedule and consider the needs of the children. Maybe our friends south of the border have the best idea after all with their siestas. In summary, the best thing is for the mother not to work. The next best thing is for her to cut down on her work and just work part-time. If that is not possible, then she should be able to come home sometime during the day. If this is not possible, she should have a babysitter who is like a second mother who will love the child and give it motherly care.

7. *Parents should have their own lives together.* The child should not ever sense the fact that he has come betwen Mother and Father. Regular times should be set when Mother and Dad are together alone for pleasure, recreation, conversation and romance. Psychologists who say that Mother and Dad should make love in front of the children, or for that matter even expose their bodies in front of the children, either do not know the Word of God or they do not care about its truths. They use the argument that children should become familiar with the human body, the differences between males and females, and the changes that occur as a person matures. They encourage that the parents let the children see their private parts and that they appear nude in front of the children. This is not only foolishness, but it is not Biblical! The father represents God in the home and should be treated with respect by the child. This respect is broken down when the parents, sincere though they may be, heed the wicked counsel of people who know little or care little about the Word of God and advise them to let their children see them in the nude. This was one of the sins that Ham committed

that drew God's displeasure. Parents appearing
nude in front of their children always draws God's
displeasure. These so-called child-rearing experts
say that extreme parental modesty leads a child to
develop a desire to see naked people and that this is
the way "peeping toms" are born. Nothing could
be further from the truth! This is a part of the
modern sex education trend.

The baby is here. Your lives are changed tremendously, but you must not completely consume your
time with the baby. You must be away some and
have other interests and other activities. Though
these times of absence should be brief, at least as
brief as possible, they nevertheless should be a part
of your schedule. You will always return to your
baby more refreshed and more able to care for him
properly and to express your love more beautifully.

Chapter Six

DISCIPLINING AN INFANT

The last chapter in this book covers the general subject of the discipline and punishment of children; hence, we will deal in this brief chapter only with the unique way to discipline infants. Disciplining infants is extremely difficult, but it must be done. Discipline teaches that there are limits in life and that within those limitations life can be beautiful. It must teach, however, that living outside those limitations is painful. Because of this, the parent must see to it that pain of some kind is inflicted when wrong is done—pain of loneliness, pain of being hurt because you disappointed someone you love. It may be physical pain, but the child must be taught that doing wrong hurts in some way and that the hurt that wrong brings is far greater than the enjoyment it gives. Proper discipline teaches a child to learn to accept these limitations. It must be understood that a child is going to test a parent concerning his discipline. Because of this, the parents must be consistent. The punishment for a certain crime must be consistent. Some rules to follow are:

1. *Always have the same punishment for the same crime.* The child then can associate certain types of pain to certain types of deeds. He can remember that pain that follows each deed. In other words, there is a predictability and steadiness in the punishment of a child.

2. *Always inflict the punishment for the crime.* If the child knows or feels that there are times when he can get by with committing the crime, and if

97

there is at least a possibility of his escaping the punishment, he may well choose to run the risk. However, if he comes to the conclusion that punishment is always given, he will come nearer deciding against the doing of the wrong deed.

If a child gets the idea that he has freedom of expression that will not be repressed at all, he is being given a false impression of what society will expect of him later. The parent should, by his discipline and punishment of the child, teach him what to expect in years to come. Parents must prepare him to be a law-abiding citizen. The child must be taught the boundaries of the law and the penalty received by living outside those boundaries.

Spanking should begin by the time the child is able to walk. I'm not talking about beatings, slappings, etc. I am talking about firm, but gentle and loving spankings. There are things, for example, that will endanger a child's life, such as crawling too close to the window or playing with the electrical plug. It would be far better for a child to receive the pain of a spanking than the pain of serious injury or death by being electrocuted or falling from the window.

3. *Develop a consistent pattern in your behavior.* The infant will probably repeat his actions several times. In order to establish for sure that you are responsible, always be the same. Be sure that your response is the same so that the infant will see a predictability about it.

When our children first learned to walk, I took them on a tour of the house. I pointed to certain objects and said, "No, no, no, no, no!" Again I pointed to the objects and said, "No, no, no, no, no!" I did this until the children associated the object with "No!" When I felt that they had associated the word "no" with objects they should not touch and things they should not do, I then proceeded to let them know that pain was associated with disobedience. I did not take a stick and hit the child; neither did I beat him with my fist, but lovingly and gently and tearfully I used the place that God has provided for spankings, and I gave him a spanking with whatever intensity I felt the crime demanded. The intensity should not be determined by the anger of the parents or the discomfort that the crime caused them. It should be commensurate with the crime. The parent should remember that the most important thing is to develop a close relationship with the child. I recall when my mother used to give me long talks. I would rather have had a spanking any day because the worst thing about the punishment was that Mother was displeased and that our fellowship was broken. When the parent and child have a sweet, close, intimate relationship, it enables the punishment of a breech of fellowship to be the worst punishment of all. This does not mean that the child should never be spanked. It means that even in spanking the child knows that Mother or Father is displeased.

Chapter Seven

TEACHING THE CHILD ABOUT GOD

Once a little child drew a picture. One of his parents asked him who it was he had drawn. The child replied, "That's a picture of God." The parent said, "Why, honey, no one knows what God looks like," whereupon the child replied, "They do now."

Faith comes natural to a child. The best time of his life to teach him about God is in his early days. Our Catholic friends have said for years that if they can have a child until he is seven years old, they have him for life. This is probably right. Someone has called these years the seven vulnerable years. How foolish it is for parents who have faith in God to use such philosophies as "Let the child decide for himself," "We don't want to push religion on the child," etc. During this brief period of childhood, youngsters are especially vulnerable to religious training.

Somewhere I read that a little baby goose has an unusual characteristic along this line. It is said that the first thing he sees moving near him after he is hatched, he will follow. Of course, if the mother goose is this first object, he follows her. If for any reason she leaves him, he will follow any other object. In other words, there is a time in his early life when he will attach himself to anything that moves which is near him. This is true with a child. Because of this we should seize upon the opportunities to train the child from birth.

There are several things that must be done.

1. *Teach him that there is a God and that that*

God loves him. Once a little child asked, "Mother, what does the world stand on?"

The mother stuttered timidly and replied, "The world stands . . . er . . . ah . . . on the shoulders of a big strong man."

The child waited a moment and said, "Mother, what does the man sit on?"

The confused mother stuttered a while longer and said, "Well, honey, the man stands on . . . er . . . ah . . . ah . . . on a big rock. That's right, a big rock!"

The child replied after a few moments, "Mother, what does the rock stand on?"

The bewildered mother hesitated for a moment and said, "Sweetheart, the . . . er . . . the rock . . . er . . . ah . . . the rock . . . ah . . . sits on a big pole."

The child then asked, "Mother, what does the pole stand on?"

An angry mother said, "Oh, the pole just reaches all the way down to the bottom!"

This is often the extent of training about God given to a little child. We teach him to bathe, to brush his teeth, to eat, to sleep, to develop good habits, and yet we fail to teach him about the most important thing in his life—an individual's relationship with God.

2. *It is important that a child's first impressions be of spiritual matters.* This is why it is important to pray with the child when he is still an infant. He should have impressions made quickly concerning Mom and Dad having their head bowed. Early impressions should include his parents holding a black book, going to church regularly, singing from a hymn book, etc. As soon as possible he should be taught to fold his hands and bow his head in prayer and though these things are no more

religious to him as far as his consciousness is concerned than any other gesture, he will soon associate them with regular habits, and these habits will lead him one day to know their meaning. These impressions will linger with him.

The infant should have pleasant thoughts about these impressions. He should be comfortable during them and learn to associate pleasantness with their performance. His first impressions of the church nursery should be associated with pleasantness and comfort. (This is why it is so important to have a cheerful, clean, comfortable church nursery.)

3. *The young child should be exposed to proper heroes.* Children are great to emulate other people. They make heroes and want to be like them. This is why parents should expose little children to the best patterns possible and should from childhood point them to adults whom they can emulate as their heroes.

4. *The parents should build proper respect for God's man.* Children should be taught that God has given to them a preacher. That preacher is God's man to lead them, to teach them, to preach to them, and to guide and instruct them concerning their lives. It is important for a family to have a man of God just like it is important to have a family doctor, a family dentist, etc. For that matter, it is even more important! The parents should never criticize God's man but should train their children to love and respect him.

This can be done in many ways. One of the most important ways is to lead the child to pray for the preacher many times a day. Every time he bows his head to say grace or to say his "Now I lay me" prayers, he should pray for his preacher. He should get an early impression that one of the most important persons in the world is God's man, his pastor.

The nursery workers at First Baptist Church have little bibs made for the babies. On each bib is printed, "I love my Preacher." This is very important.

The child should feel that he has a friend in the pulpit and that that friend loves him and is very wise. The time will probably come when the parents will need the pastor in the rearing of the child. It often is true that a time comes when the only hope of saving the child is the pastor. If the parents have been critical of him or have a negative attitude toward him, the children will develop such an attitude and will not come to the pastor when they need him in a period of crisis.

5. *From infancy the child should be taught that Jesus is the Son of God and that the Bible is the Word of God.* When I was an infant my mother started a little ritual. Every night she would put me on her knee, hold her Bible in front of me and say, "Son, the Bible is the Word of God." Then she would ask me to repeat after her those words. Three times she would do this. Then she would tell me that Jesus is the Son of God. I would have to repeat it after her. Again she would say it and again I would repeat it. A third time she would say it and a third time I would repeat it. She then told me that I should always believe those two great truths. Now I do not recall when she started it; I do know she started this practice long before I could comprehend what was going on, but as far back as I can remember I can see my mother teaching me that Jesus is God's Son and that the Bible is God's Word.

She would then mention some kind of sin and warn me concerning its evil. One night she would take a whiskey ad. She would hold it up before me and say, "Whiskey—bad, bad, bad, bad! Whiskey—bad, bad!" Then I was required to say, "Whiskey—bad, bad.' " She would then get a frown on her face, tear up the ad, throw it on the floor and stomp on it. She would shout, "WHISKEY—NO, NO! WHISKEY—BAD, BAD!" Mother was trying to associate bad words with whiskey. I do not know when she started this. I do know it was before I realized it, and the association between the words "whiskey" and "no" made a lasting impression on my mind and life.

6. *The wise parent will act out Bible stories.* For our children I would take a Bible story like "The Good Samaritan." I would be the man who was attacked. I would rock and reel like I had been attacked. I would then lie down like the man beside the road. I would then become the priest and Levite who came by and looked on him. Then I would come by and be the good Samaritan. I made it as interesting as possible. This was a regular ritual at bedtime at our house. As long as our children were small they looked forward to Dad telling them stories from the Bible and acting them out.

Once a little girl was being told the story, "The Good Samaritan," by her Christian worker. The teacher described how the man had been beaten, stripped of his raiment, was lying there bloody and hurt. Then she asked her class, "Girls, what would you have done if you had seen a man in that shape?"

A little girl said, "I would have thrown up!"

Stories are real to little children. One of the best ways to train a child is to take Bible stories and truths and teach them night after night and day after day.

7. *As soon as possible the child should be taught to memorize Scripture.* Start off with simple ones

like, "God is love," "Be ye kind one to another,"
etc. As soon as possible, teach verses that are more
difficult. It is very important that a child be taught
to memorize the Word of God in the early days of
his life.

8. *The father image is very important in teaching
the child about God.* The father is God's representative. God calls Himself our Heavenly Father and
then gives a father to each home. The child should
respect, revere and love that father. When he hears
of his Heavenly Father he will find it easy to respect
and obey Him. This means that the child's earthly
father should do his best to emulate the Heavenly
Father. For the child who has a Christian father,
his thoughts of God are those of being a man, for
the Christian father is the nearest thing on earth to
God to the little child.

9. *The infant should be taught to respect authority.* This means all authority. When he is taught to
obey every authority such as his father, his mother,
his Sunday school teacher, his baby sitter, etc., it
will not seem difficult for him to obey God when he
hears and understands the plan of salvation.

10. *The father should punish the child for doing
wrong, even as the Heavenly Father punishes His
children for doing wrong.* In infancy this punishment should not be associated with the Heavenly
Father, but the law of sowing and reaping can be
taught in infancy and early childhood. Since the
father is God's image and representative in the
home, he should, of course, act as much like the
Heavenly Father as possible. As the Heavenly
Father punishes wrong, so should the earthly father
punish wrong. As this punishment breaks the heart
of the Heavenly Father, even so it should break the
heart of the earthly father. As this punishment
from the Heavenly Father is prompted by love,

even so should the punishment from the earthly father be prompted by love.

Perhaps there is no better way for the child to learn about God than for him to have the proper relationship with his father. Respect for God's deputy in the home will lead to respect for God and to an early conversion.

Chapter Eight

EXPRESSING LOVE TO YOUR CHILD

For most of my days at home, I was the only child. Lorene was the first child; she was afflicted. Lorene never walked or talked; in fact, she never got out of bed. She lived to be seven, and at that age, God took her to Himself.

The second child was a little girl named Hazel. Hazel was in every way a normal child. When she was seven she had a serious case of the measles and appeared to be well. Suddenly, however, there was a relapse and God took her to Heaven to be with Lorene.

The third child was Earlyne, my sister, who is eight years my senior and who is now Bursar at Hyles-Anderson College. When I was a young boy, Earlyne married. Not long after that, my father left us, and Mother and I were left to live together. Maybe it was because I was the only boy, maybe it was because Mother's two oldest children went to Heaven at the age of seven, or maybe it was because of my father turning to alcohol and leaving home that caused my mother to be very loving and affectionate to me. I do not ever recall as a child going to bed at night without my mother saying, "I love you, son." I do not ever recall to this day ever being at my mother's or with my mother for a small period of time without hearing her say, "I love you, son," as we parted. I am assuming in this chapter that you do love your child. There are millions of parents who sincerely love their children who are unable to convey that love. There are several ways that love can be expressed.

1. *Express your love with words.* Start at birth saying, "I love you." Let it be one of the first things that registers in the mind of the child. Let it be one of the first sentences the child learns to say. These "I love you's" should be appropriate. When the child is an infant, this poses no problem, for an infant cannot be embarrassed by such treatment. However, as the months and years pass, the verbal expressions of love should be fitly spoken at appropriate times and in appropriate ways. It should always be said at bedtime. For the smaller child it should be said when he goes out to play. It can be said later as the child leaves for school. The wise parents will be careful, however, when the child grows older to become more private with their verbal expressions of love.

It must be remembered that when a child comes into the world his first impressions are through feelings. As soon as he begins to talk, he soon learns to ask the question, "Do you love me?" He is grasping for affection.

2. *Express your love with physical contact.* Words are wonderful, but they are not enough. I John 3:18, "My little children, let us not love in word, neither in tongue; but in deed and in truth." When the infant has physical contact with his parents, he has a tremendous urge to be cuddled, held, hugged and kissed. It is tragic but true that most parents do very little of this, especially as the infant becomes a small child and as the small child becomes a bigger child and as the bigger child becomes an adolescent. As the little child grows older, the touch of the parent is basically given only when necessary, such as when dressing the child, putting him into his high chair, helping him into the car, etc. The wise parent will find ways of giving physical contact to his child. When the stage of infancy

is over, the cuddling and "gooey" physical contact should transfer into a more casual behavior for a boy than for a girl. For a boy, the contact should be diminished gradually, and as he becomes an older child, such affection in front of others should be almost eliminated. When our son, David, was a boy, I would poke him in the ribs, tassel his hair, slap him on the knee, pat him on the back, trip him as he walked down the hall, "accidentally on purpose" bump into him as we met, etc. In times of serious conversation, I would place my hand casually on his shoulder. This was not seemingly a planned kind of a thing as far as he was concerned. It was casual and apparently nonchalant.

As he became older, his needs for physical affection such as hugging and kissing lessened. However, he still needed physical contact. I turned to such methods as jostling, boxing, giving bear hugs, wrestling, etc. These physical contacts were never showy or obvious but were relaxed and natural.

For the daughters, the physical expressions were different. Of course, as infants there was the same type of "goochie-goo" that I gave to David. I would pat them on the cheek, touch them on the shoulder, lightly touch the hand, arm or shoulder. I might even place my arm around a daughter with a half joking little pull or jerk toward me. I might slip up behind one of the girls and put my hands over her eyes and say, "Guess who!" in a disguised voice. I would maybe casually hold her hand as we strolled down the sidewalk, and in more tender moments I would gently kiss her on the cheek with a soft, "I love you," whispered into her ear.

While a boy's desire for the affectionate type of physical contact lessens as he grows older, a girl's increases, and her need for tender affection is greater. Perhaps the boy's lessens because this type of expression is considered sissy or feminine. At any rate, as David grew to around the age of 10, I gradually decreased my affectionate type of physical contact, while during the same years I increased this show of affection to the girls. Bear in mind, I gave David this affection in abundance when he was an infant. It is sad but true that infant girls under the age of one receive much, much more affection than infant boys. This should not be the case. Maybe this accounts for the fact that many times more boys need psychiatric help than do girls. The wise parent will use physical contact to express love to his small child. It must be noted, however, that this physical contact should decrease sharply as the child approaches adolescence in the case of mother to son and father to daughter.

3. *Express your love with time.* Each parent should spend time alone with each child. Children are important. Notice how Jesus regarded them in Mark 10:13-16. Notice how important children are in Psalm 127:3-5. Because each child is important, then each one should feel that he is a specially designed gift from God. He needs individual attention from the parent. Gifts, ice cream and candy, etc. will not take the place of time. It is very important that a child have definite personal attention given to him. Find time to be alone with him. Let this time be free from distractions. Let it be his time. Many times when the children were small, I made appointments with them. When others would seek my attention at that time, I would not grant it to them. I would say that I had an appointment. I realize that finding time to be alone with each child is difficult, but the good parent will find such time. This special treatment when parent and child are alone together giving their undivided attention to each other, will be sacred. The child will never

forget it as the memories grow sweeter with the passing of the years.

With our urban society, it is extremely difficult to give time to each child. We only have 7 days a week, 24 hours a day, and 60 minutes to the hour. This means that it is impossible for one to fulfill all of his obligations. Hence, it becomes a matter of priorities. This is where your child fits in. He must be given some time! It will not take a lot of time. It just takes a small amount of time which is all his. He must feel that there is nothing else you want to do, and he must feel that he is very special. It must be time spent with him alone. This is a critical need in the life of every child.

One of the dangers with the kind of relationships we are talking about is the possibility of developing a possessiveness which means the child is too dependent upon the parents. Before a child is born, he totally dependent upon his mother. When he is 4 and 5 years of age, he is 90% dependent. When he is 6 and 7 years of age, he is approximately 75% dependent. When he becomes 9-12 years of age, he is about 50% dependent. In his early teen years, he is about 25% dependent. When in high school he is about 10% dependent. Notice that he is gradually through the years becoming independent. Now while we are attempting to be close to him, we must of necessity realize that he is going through a process of leaving us. Hence, we must not smother the child, but we should give him some time that is all his.

Another danger with parents who spend time with their children is the danger of trying to live their lives through their children. In other words, the mother leads her daughter to do what the mother herself has always wanted to do or what she tried to do and failed to do. This often happens with the father. This is a form of over-possessiveness where the father identifies with the son or the mother identifies with the daughter in an effort for the child to succeed where the parent failed. This is very dangerous. The father could want to make his son perform athletic feats which he himself could not perform. The mother could wish to live vicariously through her daughter's educational life or even romantic life.

The wise parent will give the child some time that is his own, and when natural separation takes place, the parent may perform it graciously and admirably to the child's happiness with the new mate's gratitude, and the parent will have some justifiable feeling of accomplishment.

4. *Love the reluctant child too.* There are some children who resist receiving affection; that is, they resist the usual ways that parents give love. They would not like to be touched by the parent, they do not want individual attention from the parent, and they may reject verbal expressions of love. Usually they are not rejecting love; they actually WANT love but will not allow themselves to appear to like it. This child should be treated rather normally. However, since he feels uncomfortable in receiving love, or at least appears to do so, a gradual increasing in showing love is in order.

It is wise for parents not to demonstrate love at times when the child obviously prefers not to receive it. It may manifest itself when the parent is obviously planning to give affection. For example, suppose the parent has planned a time for being alone with the child and the child gets the idea that it is going to be a love-making time; he then builds up a resistance. Often a child refuses love when he is not well. This also is a time when he knows the parent is going to offer it. The child knows that it is the time to receive love. He knows that this is a good time for his parents to come to his rescue and demonstrate their affection. Now since these are usual times of expression, he openly rebels against them. He wants these tender moments to be spontaneous, unique to him. He may even feel that the parent feels obligated to show his love and that it is not sincere.

(All of us have a little bit of this resistance in us when it is the time expected for people to do something kind for us. Many of us would rather have attention for no seeming reason which comes because of spontaneity.)

To conquer this problem, the parent should try not to be predictable in showing his love. He must win the child's confidence by spontaneously at different times expressing love. Gradually, the child can become confident of the sincerity of his expressions. He will then accept affection at the traditional times also.

All children need these natural ways of receiving love. They need special attention, they need physical contact, they need to be loved when emotionally upset, when ill, when victorious, on their birthdays, at Christmastime, etc., but often they will not receive it because it is the time expected of parents to give it. Of course, a normal parent is going to want to show affection at the traditional times. This will develop later if the parent is patient by starting gradually with little surprising, spontaneous displays and gradually increasing until the child is happy to accept the parent's affection in its completeness.

Chapter Nine

QUESTIONS AND ANSWERS

Following are a few of the questions that have been asked me through the years concerning the rearing of infants:

QUESTION: Is it better to teach children in a group or on a one-to-one basis?

ANSWER: A child who early in life does not develop deep one-to-one relationships often has difficulty developing these relationships in adulthood. This is why it is better for a child to grow up in a home than in an institution; that is, if the home is what it ought to be. In institutional living, the child relates to many people but without close contact to any one individual. Children raised in institutions often are delightful people, but they have not been trained in giving themselves to an individual and to a meaningful relationship.

Though I do believe that families should spend some time together, I also believe that every parent should spend time alone on a regular basis with each child in order that he may get to know him as an individual. Susanna Wesley, the famous mother of John and Charles Wesley, did this. Though she had many children, she gave each one an hour a week when she taught him and trained him. It is, I think, very important that even in infancy this one-on-one relationship be established. Not only should there be times when Mother and Father and all the children get in the car and go somewhere or fellowship in a room together, it is also important that each child get to know each parent in a personal way.

114

QUESTION: What is the most important need in a parent's personality?

ANSWER: Consistency! It is vitally important that the parent be consistent in his reactions if the baby is to learn properly. The baby learns from each situation that he encounters. His mind records parental response. It is vital that this parental response be consistent. Suppose, for example, that he points his finger to you and says, "No, no, no, no, no!" and the first time he does it, you laugh. Then the next time he does it you become angry. Then your child will have to test you again and again in order to see which reaction will be the most prevalent one.

Suppose one time he throws his cup on the floor. You smile because you are in a good mood, and very lovingly you say, "Don't do that again." Then the next time he throws the cup on the floor in the same manner, he wants another smile. This time you are not in such a good mood. You become angry. You spank him on the hand, and scold him vehemently. The child has no way to record a consistent pattern of behavior on your part. He may continue throwing the cup on the floor until he finds what your usual reaction is going to be. In other words, it confuses the child when the parent acts inconsistently. The child needs to know what his behavior will do to you and what kind of response each action on his part will bring from you. The truth is, your baby is a research scientist, and you are his laboratory. He is studying to find out what responses you will give to various stimuli. This little scientist will discontinue his experiment when he finds a definite trend. Hence, it is tremendously important that the parent be predictable and consistent in his behavior and his response.

QUESTION: Pastor, I am expecting a baby, but I am not married. Should I keep the baby or place it for adoption?

ANSWER: There is no set answer to this question. There are, however, a few guidelines by which I go in counseling unmarried expectant mothers.

1. If you love the baby's father and he loves you, and you want to marry and you are mature enough to marry, then do so.

2. If you are not mature enough to marry (seek wise counsel about this), then do not let the fact that you are pregnant lead you to the marriage altar. One mistake doesn't correct another, and two wrongs don't make a right!

3. Do not marry just to give the baby a name and a father. Sometimes the girl's parents rush their daughter and the young man involved to the altar in order to save face. The two marry so the baby will not be born without a mother and father who are married to each other. As soon as the baby comes, separation comes and soon, there's a divorce. This type of convenient marriage doesn't save face and is not wise; in fact, it is not right! People should marry for love, not because of obligation.

4. If it is impossible according to the aforementioned guidelines for you to marry, then I would suggest that you place the baby for adoption. Contact a godly pastor. He will have people in his church, or in his acquaintance, who for some reason cannot have children. The pastor and the couple may contact an attorney who can make legal arrangements according to the laws of the particular state involved. In such a situation, the unwed expectant mother should not know now or ever who the adoptive parents are. The adopting parents should pay for the legal expenses, the hospital bill,

the doctor bill, and if possible, even provide money anonymously for maternity clothing for the unwed expectant mother.

This kind of advice is not very popular today with all the illegitimate children there are, but it is far better for the baby to have a Christian father and mother and a good, solid home than to grow up in a situation where there is no father and where soon he will learn that he is an illegitimate child and that his mother conceived him in sin. People sometimes argue with this advice, but they don't have to see the child at school filling out the form that says, "Father's name." They don't attend the first piano recital and hear the other children say, "Where is your father?" They do not see the child as he grows up having to answer on questionnaires and application forms hundreds of times the name of his father and there is no name to put there. (Every reader would agree with this writer if he had had the experience that I have had in dealing with such cases.)

QUESTION: At what age should I put my child in the church nursery?

ANSWER: Put him there as soon as you, Mother, are strong enough to come to church. Usually this would be within two weeks. The child should get the idea immediately that there is a big building that you go to every week. His little mind thinks, "Some real nice people see me there. Those real nice people all have big black books with them and they seem so happy." These things should register in the child's mind as soon as possible.

Yes, I know that all the church nurseries aren't as clean as they should be, but all of your houses aren't as clean as they should be either. Take the child to God's house, and put him in the nursery the first Sunday and every Sunday when the parents are able to attend.

QUESTION: When is a child old enough to be spanked?

ANSWER: This is a disputed question. I will tell you what has been done to our children. I spanked them as soon as they were able to walk. This may be as early as nine months. In the case of our children, it was nearer to a year. When I say spank, I do not mean slap, hit, attack, or beat, I mean, spank. I recommend using the open hand on the child's little bottom.

In my book, HOW TO REAR CHILDREN, I go into great detail explaining how to spank. It is, however, important for an infant to be spanked sooner after the wrong is done than for an older child. A spanking should always be associated with a crime, and the child should know that the spanking is associated with the particular wrong that he has done. Time moves much slower to an infant which means the spanking cannot be quite as planned as it is with an older child. It must be almost as soon as the crime is committed so that he may connect the wrong and the punishment.

QUESTION: What is the main reason babies cry if they are not sick or hurting?

ANSWER: Boredom! When the baby is born, he is capable of doing several things. He can feel, he can taste, he can see, he can hear, he can smell, etc. The baby has a natural desire to use these gifts called senses. If he does not have ample opportunity to use these gifts or senses, he becomes bored.

When babies become bored, they show their boredom by crying, and they usually cry until somebody does something to alleviate the boredom. This means the baby should have sufficient toys, attachments to his crib and, yes, even attention from the parents to keep him from being bored.

QUESTION: Is it true that a child cannot see until he is six weeks old?
ANSWER: Absolutely not! The child can see his mother while he is still at the hospital, and no one can disprove this.

QUESTION: Is an infant's smile caused by gas?
ANSWER: Absolutely not! An infant smiles because he is happy or pleased. He may smile at his mother immediately. Do not forget that the infant is a human being; so I am; so are you. Having gas on the stomach doesn't make me smile; it doesn't make you smile; and it doesn't make a baby smile. It may be the baby will smile at the very moment there is gas, but this does not mean the gas causes a smile. A baby is human. He smiles like any other human. He smiles because he is pleased or happy or because he loves you or is expressing that love.

QUESTION: I have an adopted child. When and how should I tell him that he is adopted?
ANSWER: By all means, tell him. Start when he is a little child telling him that there are two ways mothers and fathers get babies. One is that God brings them into a home and they stay there. The other is that God sometimes lets parents go to another home and choose their baby. Make this last

method seem very appealing to the child. Keep teaching it to him until he is five or six years of age. Tell him that you were very fortunate in that you got to choose your baby. Let him know that he was born of someone else but that God gave him to you for a special reason. Handled properly, the child can feel even more loved than the one naturally born.

QUESTION: I am a mother rearing a child alone. What can I do to substitute for my child not having a father?
ANSWER: My mother faced the same problem. I can tell you how she solved it. She chose men whom she admired and whom she wanted me to emulate, and she let them be a father-image to me. She pointed them out and told me what qualities they had. She would ask me to see what qualities I thought they had that were good. We discussed them, and she told me that was what she wanted me to be like when I became a man.

She would often talk to one of these men and ask if he could be a little bit close to me.

She also saw to it that I was around masculine men. She encouraged me to participate in sports so that I would be around coaches and men that are athletic. In other words, she encouraged me to get to know masculine men, to be around them. Then in a subtle way, they helped me.

QUESTION: What can I do to prevent my child from becoming a homosexual or a lesbian?
ANSWER: There is not one definite answer to your question, but there are a few things worth remembering. First, I would suggest that little boys

play with little boys, and that little girls play with little girls. This not to say that little boys should never play with little girls, and that little girls should never play with little boys. It is to say that by far the majority of a child's playing should be with his own sex. So much of the sex drive is caused by the unknown. If a little boy plays with other little boys, there will be a mystique about girls, but if he plays with little girls too much, they will become commonplace and there will be a mystique toward little boys. The human race is so constructed that when something becomes commonplace, it is not nearly as attractive to us. The old adage, "The grass is greener on the other side of the fence," applies here. In childhood this grass on the other side of the fence should be the opposite sex. If it is one's own sex, there would be a curiosity about that. Now I'm aware that the modern psychologists will say, "Let little boys see little girls, and let little girls see little boys, and let them become acquainted with the biological differences, and let them see each other unclothed." Let me remind you that that same generation of modern psychologists is turning out an unbelievable amount of homosexuals in our country!

The wise parents of a little boy will teach him that the body of a little girl is sacred, and they will see to it that he plays with other little boys. As he grows older, this mystique will follow its normal course, and he will be attracted to the opposite sex or "the grass on the other side of the fence."

One of the best ways of doing this is to lead the boy to develop interests that are masculine. This means his hobbies, his activities and his interests should be masculine to the extent that it will require him to be around other boys. The same is true for little girls developing feminine interests. (Please obtain and read the author's booklet, "Is the Homosexual Sick or Sinful?" It will throw added light on your question and its answer.)

QUESTION: Does my child hate discipline?

ANSWER: Quite to the contrary! Children actually like discipline; they enjoy it. Life is more predictable when parents set rules and enforce them with consistency. Children like things that are predictable and that have pattern. There is also security in having boundaries set by strong leadership.

Quite often a teenager will come to me and ask me if I will spank him. When I ask him why, he says, "My mother and dad never spanked me. I wish someone loved me enough to spank me now."

Of course, this discipline must come from loving parents to children who trust them. When the child learns to trust Mom and Dad, he will be glad for the boundaries they set, for he will know it is for his own good. This discipline, regardless of what shape it takes, should teach the child, even in infancy, that doing wrong brings discomfort and not comfort and that the pain of doing wrong is far greater than its enjoyment.

All over America today older people with nothing wrong with them are lying in rest homes forsaken and forgotten. There are those for whom it is best to be in such an environment, but there are tens of thousands of these dear older people who, because their children do not want to bother with them, are placed in these homes. These are the parents who did not have a close relationship with their children and/or who did not punish them for wrong. They helped to teach their children irresponsibility. Now that the children have grown up and the parents have grown old, the sons and daughters lack the responsibility to take care of their obligation toward the ones who reared them.

QUESTION: What are the most important things to remember as I discipline my child?

ANSWER: First, always warn the child in advance of what the punishment will be for his wrong. This warning can be by telling him if he is old enough. If he is not old enough, he must learn it by the consistent and predictable punishment meted out by the parents. This is what makes punishing infants so difficult. You can't tell a one-year-old child in advance what the punishment will be for his wrongdoing, but he must be taught the pain of doing wrong. This is where spanking enters. A child must be spanked when he gets close to danger. You can't tell a child who is 11 months old that he will be electrocuted if he plays with a wall socket. You cannot tell him that he will fall out of a window and kill himself if he crawls near the windowsill. It is far better to give spankings than to endanger his life.

The pseudo child psychologist will preach from the housetops against spanking a child; he would do better to realize that it is better for a child to have a little physical discomfort on his bottom end than to be lying dead. Self-styled experts had better understand that it is more child abuse to risk the child's chances of being electrocuted than to sting his bottom a little bit in teaching him not to play with a wall plug. There are those (who, by the way, have never successfully reared a decent child) who believe that anything a child does willfully should be accepted and that he is only expressing his feelings, and if we limit him in his behavior, it will cause frustrations in his personality. Nothing could be farther from the truth! The child *should* be frustrated in his attempt to do wrong! When he is old enough to walk around, he is ready for discipline, punishment and, yes, spanking. He will be a lot less frustrated concerning what he can and can't do.

When each of our children was about a year old, I took him on a guided tour of the house, and when he felt he wanted to go his own way, I gently but sternly spanked. We didn't move the vases in our house, rearrange the furniture or take the pictures off the walls. We are reminded in holy Scripture, "Whom the Lord loveth He chasteneth." Hence, chastening should be an expression of love.

Suppose a child tears a paper. Scold him when he tears it the first time. When he tears it again, include a mild spanking and a disturbed "No." If he tears it again, react in the same way. In a while the child will get the idea that the parent is consistent, always rendering the same punishment for the same crime. This same procedure may have to be carried out about many, many things until the child knows and can see that a pattern has been set.

When David was a little boy, he would throw his chocolate milk on the floor. He turned over the chocolate milk and laughed as it spilled on the floor. I reacted firmly with both displeasure and punishment that he shouldn't do it. He enjoyed seeing the floor colored with a chocolate color. Following this deed that caused this enjoyment was a painful punishment. He finally got the idea that the enjoyment was not worth the pain. He was convinced that seeing a chocolate covered floor through tears with a hurting bottom was not as much fun as he thought it was.

He then looked at the chocolate milk, looked at me and I was still frowning. I raised my hand as if to punish him again. He then said, "No, no, no, no!" He took the chocolate milk and held it in his hand and did not spill it. Immediately a smile came across my face, and I hugged him and told him how proud of him I was. He soon discovered that restraint was more fun that yielding to his temptation. He discovered that his dad was consistent and predictable and that the pleasure from his dad's smile and loving gestures was more fun than a chocolate covered floor.

If the child is allowed to do things that are destructive or dangerous without seeing the obvious displeasure of his parents, he will continue with his wrongdoing.

Some parents who find punishing and spanking unpleasant to their own taste remove every object in the house that they think could cause trouble and thereby preserve the child from ever facing a situation where he could do wrong. Because of this, the child is never taught to control his own appetites, to discipline his own taste, and to learn self-control. It is far better to have him find the little pain that comes with little wrong when he is little than to leave him undisciplined and have him know later the big pain that comes from big wrong when he is big and then finally have him know the eternal pain that comes from the eternal wrong of rejecting Christ when he is in eternity!

QUESTION: Just exactly what does it mean in Proverbs 22:6 when the Lord says, "Train up a child in the way he should go; and when he is old, he will not depart from it"?

ANSWER: In the original language, the word for "train up" has to do with the inside of a mouth. To be quite frank, it compares a child with a horse, and his training is compared to the use of a bridle placed in his mouth. James 3:3, "Behold, we put bits in the horses' mouths, that they may obey us; and we turn about their whole body." An untamed or untrained horse has a bridle put in his mouth. That bridle is used by the trainer to teach the horse to obey him in the way the trainer would have the horse to go. Just as the horse trainer brings the horse into submission to the will of the trainer, even so it is our job to train up a child so that he will submit himself to the will of God.

QUESTION: What influence does television have on an infant?

ANSWER: Researchers tell us that very young children watch television for ¼ of their waking hours. This limits the growth of a child's brain capacity! It makes him more restless and fussy. It is too noisy and stimulating. It has contributed largely to the changing pattern of behavior among our children. It also takes him away from one of the most important things of childhood and that is reading. I would suggest that if a child is allowed to watch television at all, it be for not more than one hour a day and that the program be carefully chosen by the parent.

QUESTION: During the nine months of pregnancy, what are some things the expectant mother can do?

ANSWER: In general, be as happy as possible. Avoid tension and strife. Be as calm as possible. Live by a planned, disciplined schedule. Think happy thoughts. Read good books, and enjoy the days of waiting. I do not know how much is translated from mother to baby during pregnancy, but I do know that such habits will make for a better mother.

(Much of the material throughout this manuscript pertains to the preparation of the mother for baby's arrival.)

QUESTION: What are some negative attitudes that develop in the heart and mind of the new mother?

ANSWER: The new mother may become unsure of herself. She may feel a sense of inadequacy. Then a new mother may even feel resentment. Up until now her time has been her own. She has been free to go and come. She has not been tied down. Suddenly this freedom has been taken away from her, for the little one demands most of her attention. During pregnancy the mother should be aware of these possible reactions and prepare for them.

This resentment could come because of a false assumption that the baby will draw the mother closer to her husband. Then she finds that this little peacemaker can become a divider, and instead of bringing them together, the newborn can become a wedge to separate them. This possibility should be realized and preparation during pregnancy should be made.

QUESTION: What are some negative things that can enter into the father's mind?

ANSWER: The father could become jealous of the attention his wife gives the new baby. His wife's total life has belonged to him. Now she has so much responsibility for the child, and he may feel abandoned. These possibilities must be considered.

The couple must not only prepare for them, but the young mother must give extra attention to the husband, and both of them must work hard to be close during these important days.

QUESTION: What is the most important thing for a father to be?

ANSWER: The most important thing for the father to be to the child is a good image. The first idea that the child has concerning what God is like is that of his father. He has never seen God; consequently, his earthly father is an image of his Heavenly Father. Because of this, the earthly father must be as near as possible what the Heavenly Father is. One day the child will know the Heavenly Father in a personal relationship, but until he is old enough to transfer that image, his father is God to him. Now don't misunderstand me. The father is not in a real sense God, but the father represents God and has power of attorney from the Heavenly Father, and he is to present God's image to the child.

QUESTION: At what age should the parent begin teaching the Bible to the child?

ANSWER: I taught the Bible to each of our children as soon as he was home from the hospital. Every night I would tell a Bible story. I would act it out. I would take stories like "Jonah and the Whale," "David and Goliath," "Daniel in the Lion's Den," etc. and tell the entire story using such things as pantomime, monologue, etc. I did this practically every night at bedtime from the time the children were a week old.

QUESTION: At what age should the child be taught the plan of salvation?

ANSWER: I taught our children the plan of salvation regularly from the time they came home from the hospital. Now I do not know when such truths begin to register in the mind of a child. Since I do not know when, I want to be sure I am telling the child the truth of God and the way to Heaven when that time does arrive.

QUESTION: What are the consequences in failing to discipline?

ANSWER: Hebrews 12:8, "But if ye be without chastisement, whereof all are partakers, then are ye bastards, and not sons." What this verse really says is that an undisciplined child is like an illegitimate child. Because he is not disciplined, he will feel like he belongs to no one and will have the feeling that he is illegitimate. Disciplining with love and consistency gives the child security of sonship and true parenthood.

QUESTION: What are the basic needs of the infant?

ANSWER: Food, sleep, love, expressions of that love, exercise, and freedom from boredom. (For a small infant, exercise is very limited since he is confined to the swinging of the arms and legs. This means that the child should not be covered too heavily and that the room should be kept at a warm temperature so the child can have freedom of movement.)

QUESTION: What is the most common mistake concerning the house itself?

*ANSWER:*The house is too often designed for adults and not for children. When the child comes, he should be given a room if at all possible that is designed for him. Then the house should take on a new atmosphere. A person should be able to go into any room in the house and realize a child lives there.

QUESTION: Are the child's adult years affected by what happens during the first year of his life?

ANSWER: Definitely! The impact of a child's first year on his adult behavior has been documented again and again. For him to be a well established child in his first year with his emotional needs satisfied will help give him emotional stability during his adolescence and adulthood. Meeting these first-year emotional needs, however, is a great task which requires time and patience. The parent must learn to see the world through the baby's eyes. The parent must realize that the newborn baby is not a vegetable; he is a human being, and the foundation is being laid for an entire life.

QUESTION: Does a baby require extended care by his parents?

ANSWER: Extended care is not as important as the kind of care. The baby needs to feel, even by instinct, a sense of self-esteem. When this is established along with emotional security during the first year of a child's life, it will help him throughout the rest of his life.

QUESTION: Should the mother of an infant ever work?

ANSWER: There is no ironclad answer to this question. My answer would be, "No, unless it is necessary for the mother to help in the making of the living or if the mother is rearing the child alone, such as in the case of a widow, etc." In other words, there are circumstances that would require the mother to work during her child's infancy. This should not be done, however, just to drive a nicer car, buy a nicer home, buy nicer furniture, or enjoy more luxuries in life than could be enjoyed if the mother were at home.

QUESTION: If the mother works, should the father help in caring for the baby, doing housework and other duties which are normally wifely ones?

ANSWER: If both the husband and wife have full-time jobs, then they should share the work at home. The wife, for example, could do the cooking and the washing of the dishes, and the husband could do the laundry and some of the housework. The Bible plan is for man to make the living and the woman to do the housework. If, however, the woman must share in the making of the living, then the man should share in the work at home; that is to say, if the woman must help the man do his part, then the man should help the woman do her part.

QUESTION: Is traveling harmful to a baby or small child?

ANSWER: Usually it is not. Babies seem to adapt easily, and as long as safety rules are adhered to strictly, it should not hurt the baby. It is a good idea, however, to take baby's familiar objects along on the trip. Of course, Mom and Dad are most familiar to him, but he should have his own blanket, pillow, toys, etc. so as to make the car, train or plane as much like home as possible and give a homey atmosphere even to a motel room.

It is also a good idea to keep the baby on schedule as much as possible. Travel changes the baby's routine. The wise parent will try to keep the baby as near to his schedule as possible.

QUESTION: How can I alleviate the baby's fear of going to the doctor?

ANSWER: Make going to the doctor a delightful experience by having some enjoyable things to do on the same trip. Teach the child that going to the doctor is associated with a fun time on the way and returning. The parent could make the trip to the doctor a venture which includes going by the park to swing or going by the amusement park for a few minutes and getting something to eat or drink that the child enjoys. Whatever activities that are chosen should be limited to this one venture—that of going to the doctor. Then the child can delight in the trip to the doctor, and the particular day chosen for this trip can bring a smile instead of a frown to his face.

Chapter Ten

DISCIPLINE AND PUNISHMENT

A generation ago child psychologists came out with the theory that spanking a child may leave him with inner rebellion. They proposed that his desires should not be thwarted. Child psychology courses emphasized this theory. Unconverted professors and Bible-rejecting lecturers joined with misguided authors in spreading the theory that spanking a child would leave him with certain repressed desires and would thwart his progress. Sincere, but deceived parents and educators swallowed this poison. Hence, we did not spank the child's hands when he did wrong. We took the paddle out of the schoolroom and the bite out of the law. Those unspanked children are now grown. Whereas they were throwing vases in living rooms, they are now throwing stones through storefront windows. Whereas they were lighting matches in kitchens, now they are setting fires to shopping centers, R.O.T.C. buildings, and banks. Whereas they were holding baby brothers hostage in basements, they are now holding principals and college presidents hostage in administration buildings. Whereas they were rebelling against mothers and fathers, now they are rebelling against God and country. Whereas parents would not force them to bathe when the could have done so, now society cannot make them bathe as adults. Because they were not forced to dress properly as children, they will not dress properly nor assume responsibility in society now.

These prophets of anarchy taught us that spanking a child would cause the child to hate the parents. Now these unspanked children, who are supposed to love their parents, embrace a philosophy whose first premise is hatred and even a willingness to kill Mother and Father, but the young folks who were spanked as children and disciplined in adolescence have a love for their aging parents that is envied by those who were deceived by these pseudo psychologists.

Headed by their messiah, who was a leading children's physician, and inspired by his disciples who led this movement in the schoolroom, the followers of this heresy accused the Bible-believers of ruling by force and not by love. They included in their gospel such foolish statements as, "I love my boy too much to whip him," etc. They refused to accept God's admonition in Proverbs 13:24, "He that spareth his rod hateth his son: but he that loveth him chasteneth him betimes." In Hebrews 12:6 we read, "For whom the Lord loveth He chasteneth, and scourgeth every son whom He receiveth." Now we face a generation of anarchy, rebellion, and yes, even revolution which has been sown in doctors' offices, classrooms, and nurseries by such tools as typewriters, office pens, and the silver tongues of orators.

Since disregarding the Word of God concerning discipline has led us to arrive at our present destination, let us seek the reversal of such a trend by examining the Scriptures and heeding them.

The Bible is clear that little children are born in sin. Psalm 51:5, "Behold, I was shapen in iniquity; and in sin did my mother conceive me." Psalm 53:8, "The wicked are estranged from the womb; they go astray as soon as they be born, speaking lies." Because of this God has given parents to children to discipline them, to spank them, and to teach them the awful results of wrong. The plain teaching of the Scripture is that the parent who disciplines his child does both child and parent a great favor. Let us notice these favors.

1. *The parent who spanks the child teaches him to have wisdom.* Proverbs 29:15, "The rod and reproof give wisdom: but a child left to himself bringeth his mother to shame." The child is taught the wisdom that sin does not pay and that it brings displeasure, discomfort, and heartache. He will learn to associate wrong with punishment and thereby flee from it.

2. *The parent who spanks his child provides himself with a happy future.* Proberbs 29:15b, ". . . but a child left to himself bringeth his mother to shame." Oh, the heartbreak endured by parents who have failed to discipline their children. Many such are decaying in old folks' homes across the nation and around the world. They sit by silent telephones and search through empty mail boxes made so by the ungrateful child whose life is bringing shame and reproach to Mother and Dad. While these lovely souls pine their hearts away in remorse, their old-fashioned counterparts enjoy security, protection, provision, and love from those whom they spanked and disciplined as children.

3. *The parent who spanks his child guarantees him a clean life.* Proverbs 20:30, "The blueness of a wound cleanseth away evil: so do stripes the inward parts of the belly." In other words, the parent who disciplines cleanses the child from evil character and inward sin. The child has been taught that sin brings trouble. He learns to fear and hate it. Someday he will rise and call his parents blessed.

4. *The parent who spanks his child offers for himself more opportunities for service to God.* In writing to Timothy in I Timothy 3:4, 5, Paul says

that a pastor should be one who "ruleth well his own house, having his children in subjection with all gravity; (For if a man know not how to rule his own house, how shall he take care of the church of God?)" He also disqualifies from the office of deacon one who does not control his children properly. I Timothy 3:12, "Let the deacons be the husbands of one wife, ruling their children and their own houses will." Hence, one who does not follow God's plain teaching about discipline is not qualified to hold either of the offices in the New Testament church. God will not use men who disobey Him in this vital matter. One reason God blessed Abraham so mightily is the fact that He could trust him to "command his children and his household after him," according to Genesis 18:17-19.

Eli, the high priest in the days of Samuel, forfeited great blessings from God because he did not properly discipline his sons. His two sons, Hophni and Phinehas, were both wicked men. In I Samuel 3:12-14 we have God's judgment upon him. Notice very carefully in verse 13 the words, "because his sons made themselves vile, and he restrained them not." Judgment fell upon Eli and upon his house because he did not discipline his sons.

5. *The disciplining parent adds years to the life of his child.* Exodus 20:12, "Honour thy father and thy mother: that thy days may be long upon the land which the Lord thy God giveth thee." What a favor the parent does for the child when he disciplines and spanks him! He literally adds years to his life.

6. *Such a parent guarantees his own child a happy old age.* The Bible teaches in Proverbs 22:6, "Train up a child in the way he should go: and when he is old, he will not depart from it." In other words, when the child is away from home without

the presence of the discipline of his mother and father, he will not depart from his training. He will become a happy and prosperous member of society and will be a properly adjusted adult. This Scripture should be observed very carefully. Many parents of children who have gone into deep and terrible sin comfort themselves in the fact that the child will come back because Proverbs 22:6 promises it. This is not the teaching here! The Bible never promises that a child who goes off in deep sin will come back, but rather teaches that a child reared properly will never depart from the way he has been trained. In other words, it does not say, "he will come back to what he has been taught," but rather it says, "he will not depart from what he has been taught."

7. *The parent who corrects his child will probably save the life of the child.* Proverbs 23:13 says, "Withhold not correction from the child: for if thou beatest him with the rod, he shall not die." Now at first reading we might be led to believe that the teaching of this verse is that the rod itself will not kill the child and certainly this is true if administered properly, but there is another teaching here: The child who has been spanked and taught that doing wrong brings bad results, tragedy, and punishment will less likely brawl or be killed in a car wreck because of drinking while driving. He is not as likely to die of some terrible disease caused by sin. In other words, he will be taught to live a safer life than he would have lived had he not been disciplined. Ah, how fortunate is such a one!

8. *The parent who spanks the child keeps him from going to Hell.* Proverbs 23:14, "Thou shalt beat him with the rod, and shalt deliver his soul from Hell." A child who is spanked will be taught that there is a holy God Who punishes sin and

wrong. Hence, he will learn to heed authority and obey the laws and rules. When he then hears the Word of God he will obey what he hears and will accept the Gospel as it is preached. The parent has kept his child from Hell by teaching him truths that can be learned only by discipline and the use of the rod.

9. *The spanking parent teaches his child how to equip himself better for the future, for he will obtain a better education.* When the child has been taught to respect authority, obey the rules, and keep the laws before he starts to school he then transfers this obedience and respect to his school teacher. Because of this he receives a better education, better equips himself for life, and will be of more value to society and reap a larger financial reward. Hence, the parent who disciplines his child Scripturally is putting money in his pocket and success in his future.

Many parents are willing to abide by the aforementioned principles, yet do not have the knowledge of the practical side of administering such discipline. Some practical suggestions follow:

1. *Let the child realize that you are simply representing God in the execution of the punishment.* Explain to him that parents represent God before their children and that they are ministers to execute His judgment. Psalm 103:13 says, "Like as a father pitieth his children, so the Lord pitieth them that fear Him." So God is like a father and He chooses fathers and mothers to represent Him in the punishing of little children. Let the child realize that if you as a parent do not punish him properly, you are being disobedient to God and committing the same sin the child is committing. Explain to him that you are a child of God and if you refuse to obey God in the execution of His judgment upon

your children, God will pour out His wrath upon
you. For you to be a good child of God requires
that you be a good parent to the child. Let him
understand this. He will get the idea that God is a
holy and just God, One Who loves and yet One
Who wants us to become our best. For this to be so
He must punish us when we are deserving.

2. *Sometimes spanking should leave stripes on
the child.* Proverbs 20:30 says, "The blueness of a
wound cleanseth away evil; so do stripes the inward
parts of the belly." Our natural man rebels at such
punishment, but we are reminded in I Corinthians
2:14 that the natural man cannot understand the
things of the Spirit. Hence, we have to trust the
God Who knows more than we and obey Him.

I can well recall when I was a boy we had a peach
tree in the back yard. I do not ever recall seeing a
peach grow on that tree. When I think of the old
peach tree I think of Mother walking back from it
with a branch in her hand, peeling the leaves off as
she came. I then recall her using that switch to
spank my little bare legs. I can still see the stripes
often left by that switch, and I thank God for every
one of them. Today I call her "blessed" because of
her faithfulness to the teaching of God and her willingness to obey Him. Placing stripes on me as a
child kept me from bearing more painful ones as an
adult. Ephesians 6:4 says, "And, ye fathers . . .
bring them up in the nurture and admonition of the
Lord." The word "nurture" means "chastening."
It is the same word that is used concerning the
scourging of Christ as He was beaten with the cat-
o'-nine-tails. The wise and spiritual parent obeys
God and follows His commandments, not his own
reason.

3. *Begin early in spanking the child.* Susannah
Wesley said she spanked John and Charles before

they were a year old. Certainly the wise parent will start by at least this age. Proverbs 19:18 says, "Chasten thy son while there is hope, and let not they soul spare for his crying." This means there is a time in a child's life when no hope is left. During the formative years, yea, the infant years, the child should be spanked. As soon as he is old enough to walk away from his parents he should be spanked if he does not walk where they say he should walk. As soon as he is old enough to understand what they say, he should be spanked if he disobeys what they say. This Scripture admonishes us that even when a child is so young that his crying reaches our sympathy, and though it is hard for us as compassionate parents to spank one who seems so innocent, we should nevertheless discipline him. Parents should not have to remove vases and delicate glass ornaments from living room tables. A house need not become disorderly and full of riots because a baby has come. Start early in disciplining the child.

4. *The parent should build such a close relationship that the worst part of the spanking is the broken fellowship between the child and parent.* I can still recall how disappointed my Mother's face looked when she spanked me and I can recall how I dreaded displeasing her even more than I dreaded the spanking, (and believe me, I DID dread the spanking). When the love and affection is close between the child and parent and the relationship is what it ought to be, the worst part of a whipping is the broken fellowship. In other words, when the parent is not disciplining, the relationship should be so wonderful, the fellowship so sweet, and life so happy that the severance of that in itself is terrible punishment for the child to endure.

5. *The spanking should be a ritual.* No mother or father should jerk the child up and in a fit of

temper administer a spanking. In fact, no punishment should ever be given in a fit of temper. The ritual should be deliberate and last at least ten or fifteen minutes. (In the long run time will be saved using this method.) It should be a ritual dreaded by the child. He should not only dread the pain but the time consumed in the ordeal.

6. *The punishment should always be far in excess of the pleasure enjoyed by doing the wrong.* The child should realize he will always be the loser by far and that the discomfort will be so multiplied that soon he will have forgotten the pleasure derived from the wrong.

7. *The parent should state very clearly to the child the wrongs and the punishment for each one.* As near as possible these wrongs should be listed with the punishment that is to be inflicted for each one. If the punishment does not seem to correct it, then perhaps it should be increased. Some parents have made lists of possible wrongs and have carefully gone over this list with the child explaining exactly what each punishment would be. The punishment is inflicted without exception so that the child will know exactly what to expect.

8. *Before punishing the child tell him clearly what wrong he has committed.* Talk sternly and deliberately without a display of temper. Let him know exactly what he has done wrong. Then require that he state to you exactly what the wrong was so that what he did is very clear to you and to the child. Then, ask him what the punishment is. By this time he will know. Let him know that to be just and righteous you must inflict the punishment reminding him that you are doing it in the place of God against Whom he has really sinned.

9. *Never give a child that for which he cries.* The baby who cries for attention and gets it will become

a child who cries for a toy and gets it, then a teen-ager who whines and complains for his every whim and gets it, and then a young adult who will demon-strate and riot in order to get his wishes. Riots are not started in the streets but in the crib.

10. *The spanking should be administered firmly.* It should be painful and it should last until the child's will is broken. It should last until the child is crying, not tears of anger but tears of a broken will. As long as he is stiff, grits his teeth, holds on to his own will, the spanking should continue.

11. *After the spanking, tell him why you did it.* While he is still crying have him sit down. Explain to him again what the crime was and that you had no alternative but to obey God and punish him for the crime. Ask him again to repeat to you what he did that was wrong. Allow the impression of the association between the wrong and the penalty to be cut deep in his mind.

Then the wise parent should assure the child of his love and explain the reason he spanked him was because of that love. He should then have the child remain in the room alone. (All spankings should be administered in privacy and with a closed door.) The parent should have a brief prayer with the child. Lead him to realize his sin was really against God. Ask the child to pray asking God to forgive him. He should then have time to be alone in the room to think over his wrong for a few minutes. After two to five minutes the parent may open the door and allow normal activity to resume.

12. *Parents should always support each other in the disciplining of the children.* Sometimes the mother may think the father is too harsh or too mean. Sometimes the father may think the mother is illogical or unreasonable. Such feelings should never be expressed openly. (Perhaps a discussion

can be carried on privately, though in some cases this would not be advisable.)

Sometimes older teenagers say to me, "Brother Hyles, at our house we have two sets of rules: my mother's and my father's." This causes frustration in a child's life. The ideal situation would be for the mother and father to agree on what is wrong and what punishment should be inflicted. If this is not possible, there should certainly be support for each other on the part of each parent. It is always best for the parent to be on the side of authority, hence, stripping the child of his desire to seek sympathy from one parent after punishment is meted out by another.

Happy in old age is the parent who obeys God in these matters. Happy is the child who feels the security of such punishment. When Becky, my oldest daughter, graduated from high school and was preparing to go to college, I took her out to eat. I asked her how she was going to rear her children. She looked at me and said, "Dad, exactly as you have reared me." When I asked her why she replied, "Dad, I always knew you loved me when you said, 'No!' "